MARKED FOR LIFE

MARKED
for Life

Finding Grace and Grit
Where You Least Expect it

PAUL TEMPLER
REBECCA M. SIMONS

TITLETOWN
PUBLISHING

TitleTown Publishing LLC
Green Bay, Wisconsin USA

MARKED *for Life*

TitleTown Publishing, LLC
P.O. Box 12093 Green Bay, WI 54307-12093
920.737.8051 | titletownpublishing.com

Editors: Erin Walton & Tracy C. Ertl
Copy Editor: Lori Preuss
Cover Designer: Erika L. Block
Cover Image Photographer Templer: Scottie Magro
Cover Image Photographer Simons: Tiny Space Studio
Tattoo Photographer: Rebecca Marie Photography

PUBLISHER'S CATALOGING-IN-PUBLICATION DATA:

Names: Templer, Paul, author. | Simons, Rebecca M., author. **Title:**
Marked for Life: finding grace and grit where you least expect it /
Paul Templer, Rebecca M. Simons. **Description:** Green Bay, WI :
TitleTown Publishing, LLC, [2022] **Identifiers:** ISBN: 978-1-955047-
49-4 (paperback) | 978-1-955047-03-6 (eBook) **Subjects:** LCSH:
Templer, Paul. | Adventure and adventurers—Biography. | Resilience
(Personality trait) | Self-actualization (Psychology) | Self-realization.
| Conduct of life. | Spiritual life. | Spirituality. | Catastrophic
illness—Psychological aspects. | Alternative medicine. | Healing. |
Bible—Quotations. | Tattooing—Psychological aspects. | Suffering—
Personal narratives. | Bereavement. | Divorce. | Motivation
(Psychology) | Inspiration. | Faith. | Choice (Psychology) | Courage.
| Perseverance (Ethics) | Fortitude. | LCGFT: Autobiographies.
Classification: LCC: BF698.35.R47 T46 2022 | DDC: 155.24--dc23

DEDICATION

Paul

Kate, Erin, and Jack, the loves of my life. Charlie, my dog. My family and Sean my cornerstone. God, my keystone. Rebecca, my partner. Ari, Christophe, David, Donna E., Gina, Peter, Tom, and Toni, my healers. Matt and David, my fellow adventurers. Jeff, for always having my back and an eye on my future. Tracy, Debbi, Euan and Erin, for getting this book out of my head and heart and into your hands. All those I haven't mentioned by name; family, friends, friends of friends, and people all around the world who've supported and continue supporting me on this grand adventure. Thank you all, and Godspeed.

Rebecca

I have inexpressible gratitude and appreciation for those who have formed and cared for me through it all – tirelessly by Joan, filled with faith by Ted, steadfastly by Steven, into and through adulthood by Carol and Holly. I am thankful for those who have helped me to live, to Paul for fervently believing in everything, including me, and for the haven and home of Crystal Lake.

TABLE OF CONTENTS

FOREWORD

Patrick J. Kennedy

"Y ou get to choose what happens next."

Marked for Life reminded me of this universal truth, which can easily get buried in the chaos of daily life.

It's an easy concept to forget especially when you're in survival mode, navigating myriad responsibilities and concerns around family, career, finances, the pandemic, inflation, war, politics, climate change, and more every day.

The older I get the more I find myself stopping to process and course correct. It's a learned skill that I'm so very grateful for—one I haven't always had. In my youth, I frequently traveled the harder paths. Sometimes by choice and sometimes by circumstance, under the heavy weight of family tragedy, and usually in the public eye. Fear, depression, expectations, and self-doubt too often called the shots for me.

Today I am better able to take care of myself and the people, places, and things I care about. But the traumas of the past are always with me, like scar tissue. I frequently think of a Tennyson quote my father, Senator Ted Kennedy, shared in a speech back in 1980. It was one he and his brothers, President John F. Kennedy and Senator Bobby Kennedy, all loved:

> "I am a part of all that I have met
> Though much is taken, much abides
> That which we are, we are —
> One equal temper of heroic hearts
> Strong in will
> To strive, to seek, to find, and not to yield."

The world is changing and now we must change with it. I'm honored to spend my days fighting for better access to mental health and addiction care for all Americans. It's more important now than ever before. The COVID-19 pandemic has opened a lot of eyes to the realities of hardship and trauma. In fact, I feel it's led us to a critical moment in history, an awakening of sorts, where we must collectively "choose what happens next." Are we going to emerge from these challenging times better equipped to navigate life's uncertainties and take care of one another, or we will revert to old, comfortable patterns? What happens next will define a generation.

It's for this reason I'm glad *Marked for Life* emerged when it did. Through their intensely powerful and personal stories, including ones about near-death experiences and resulting emotional trauma, authors Paul and Rebecca offer insights into human strength, hope, and the ability to prevail over life's challenges. While by no means a self-help book, the pages are packed with compelling, entertaining, and relatable anecdotes that will inspire action and growth. Exactly what we need right now as the nation approaches a possible tipping point.

Brimming with theological and spiritual insights, but also steeped in neuro-literacy, *Marked for Life* will resonate with anyone who bears the scars of hardship and tragedy; anyone navigating anxiety, heartbreak, or grief; and anyone interested in changing their trajectory for the better.

Patrick J. Kennedy
Former U.S. Congressman
Founder, The Kennedy Forum

INTRODUCTION

Paul

I felt sick. Really sick. Blood was coming out of places it really shouldn't have been, my pee and poop specifically. More and more often, when I wasn't coughing, my breathing was freaking me out as it became more and more labored. I was lethargic. Most of the time, my joints, kidneys, head, and abdomen hurt, and my sometimes-confused mental state could be described as "I didn't know if I was shot, shagged, or snake bit." Sometimes I'd get really dizzy and a little confused. My memory would come and go along with my eyesight. On more than one occasion, I found myself slumped in a mucky heap on the floor… oddly; it seemed to happen most often when I was in the shower.

I stopped taking baths and cut back significantly on driving. I met and spoke with a lot of doctors, no two of whom seemed to agree on what was going on inside of me. Coupled with this, my personal life was a hot mess as my almost seventeen-year-long marriage reluctantly (at least from my perspective) gasped its terminal breaths.

I had three kids and a dog whom I liked and loved dearly, and a family and some friends who loved me too. Despite all of that, as days bled into weeks, I found I was becoming less and less attached to staying alive. If I hadn't become so incredibly disillusioned and untrusting of Western medicine, that might well have been that. A divorce process running parallel with a frustrating quest for a medical diagnosis, followed by a relatively quick ending to a life which, at least to me, had been quite an adventure.

Instead, I chose a different path.

As good a place as any to pick up the story is February 2017. It was the early days of my process of discovery. I was at the local, nationally-ranked hospital with the professionally renowned and incredibly kind head of the Nuclear Medicine Department. We were discussing my scans and her initial interpretation of them. Looking at the images in front of us, my body lit up like a Christmas tree. She worked her way through the anomalies: brain, lung, abdomen, liver, bowel, lymphatic system… the seemingly endless list went on. I struggled to stay focused on the conversation. The magnitude of what she was sharing with me only really hit home when she strongly suggested I cancel my planned business travel with great empathy and professionalism. Instead, she suggested I get my affairs in order and that I do it quickly.

As the next few days and weeks went by, the diagnoses and prognoses shifted. I was alone, afraid, and confused. One of the few things I felt I still possessed was my foolish pride; I didn't want anyone to feel sorry for me. It felt like every time I tried to speak with someone about what was going on, it was awkward. Some were awkward and great. Some were just plain old awkward. Much like well-meaning gawkers at a crash site, not knowing what to say beyond how very sorry they were whilst surreptitiously trying to find out exactly what was wrong with me.

Frustratingly I couldn't tell anyone exactly what was wrong with me. I didn't know definitively, and given the wide ranges and inconsistencies of expert opinions, my interpretations of what was going on were something I felt neither qualified, competent, nor comfortable sharing. Well, at first, it was frustrating, then it became downright irritating.

Everyone seemed to want a label to hang what was wrong with me. It felt like if I could just give everyone some names; that it was early synchronous multiple primary non-small cell lung cancer… or secondary brain tumor… or synchronous colorectal carcinomas… or multiple myeloma. If I could just throw a few letters: T denoting the size of the tumors, N for the lymph nodes with cancer, and M for whether or not they had metastasized, along with correlating numbers ranging from zero to four denoting how far and fast it had spread. Then everyone would be okay, their hyena-like appetites for information satiated. They'd kindly and well-meaningly nod their heads like they knew what I was talking about. I'd nod back at them, and we could all get on with our lives.

But as I've said, I couldn't give them what they wanted because I didn't know. And telling people that, particularly those nearest to me, wasn't working well for any of us. Suddenly, it seemed like a lot of the well-meaning people I spoke with were experts on what I might or might not have, and they had strong opinions on what I should or shouldn't be doing. So, on top of feeling scared, I was feeling more and more stupid as it felt like every time I was asked a question, I couldn't confidently answer it.

My breaking point with all of this came as a result of two seemingly unrelated events colliding. One day whilst struggling for breath, I was assured by the pulmonologist I'd just seen that everything looked fine with my lungs. It sure didn't feel that way. At around about the same time, the woman I was married to told me she wanted a divorce. I thought *You've got to be freakin' kidding me!*

It seemed to my inflamed brain and addled mind that enough was enough. Rather than continuing to wade through the overwhelmingly confusing craziness that was my life, I decided to walk away from it all.

At this point, I couldn't help but marvel at the irony of the cliché I'd become. Alanis Morisette's hit song "Ironic" would be the perfect soundtrack to the three-lane shit-show that was my life. I'd chased the American Dream. Personal and professional success, wife, kids, white picket fence, money in the bank, power, influence, right neighborhoods, vacation homes, cars, private schools, athletic clubs, clothes… blah, blah… we're all familiar with the story. In my quest to get it all, it was looking like I just might lose it all… my family, my marriage, my health… and if I listened to some of the people talking to me, there was a pretty good chance that I was going to lose my life too. It was both sardonic and infuriating. I felt stupid, and I was scared.

After feeling sorry for myself for a little while, I decided that the possibility of dying wasn't really a conversation I wanted to get too familiar with or attached to. Instead, I came up with what I thought was a fantastic idea. *To hell with Western medicine. I'm done with that. I'm off to heal, get well, and discover the meaning of life.*

What seemed to me a really good idea was met by others with responses varying from disbelief, scorn, contempt, and ridicule. Those who knew and loved me, whilst concerned, wished me Godspeed and offered their support. Those who didn't judge, ridiculed, mocked, scorned, and metaphorically clucked their tongues in disbelief. As a responsible parent, I sorted out my last will and testament then dove headlong into my marvelous healing adventure.

They say you'll never find an atheist in a foxhole; I thought I should kick this quest off by going to visit with God. Whilst I have faith that God is with me all the time and everywhere, kneeling near the spot in Jerusalem where Jesus was crucified was something else. I truly felt a connection to the Divine. Shortly thereafter, beneath the burning Israeli sun as I breathed in the dry desert air, the words *be, then do* flooded my mind, along with the absolute certainty that my path out of the illness wilderness was going to have less to do with what I did and more to do with who I was and how I was *being* whilst I *did* it.

If I was going to be a jerk living out of fear, then my chances of seeing out the year were probably slim to zip. On the other hand, if I was going to be and spread love – to myself and others – as kumbaya-esque as that sounds, the possibilities seemed infinite. Again, it may have been my brain not working the way it's designed to, but I kept on randomly thinking about tattoos and how they marked one for life. Much the same way as I felt the indelible imprint of God's love nurturing, comforting, and healing me whilst simultaneously kicking me in the arse and bidding me drive on. My next stop was exploring Kathmandu and an audience with the Karmapa Lama, trekking through the Himalayas with my good friend, Gary Guller (the first amputee to summit Mount Everest), and our merry band of Sherpas. We delivered school supplies to children in remote villages and established a social enterprise program to empower women and children who were living below the poverty line. It gave me lots of time to think, pray, listen, learn, and engage newly with myself and other people and left me in no doubt that God's fingerprints were all over this leg of my adventure.

As I flew back to the good ol' US of A, what stood out front and center and frankly struck me as quite odd, was the similarity of the responses I received in Nepal to the same line of questions I'd asked in the Holy Land. "How do I get well?" It seemed that when I stripped it all down, the Christians and the Buddhists seemed to have the same answer, "Be grateful. Be kind (to yourself and others). Just do the next right thing." This whole "Be, then do" thing was starting to make sense.

Back in the USA, I accepted that I really did need to do something about my health. Prayer and faith were great, and neither precluded doing the requisite legwork. In the interests of expediency and getting to the point... a friend of a friend was able to connect me with Dr. Tom, the principal at the New York Center of Innovative Medicine. He and his team put me through their Bioresonance Analysis of Health, an extremely comprehensive evaluation that enabled them to identify all hidden determinants of disease and dysfunction on all levels (physical, biochemical, psycho-emotional, and spiritual) and then construct a bespoke program of treatment. The results from the tests they ran correlated with and expounded upon some of the results I'd received early on what I've come to call my "Health – Scare Adventure." Particularly those I'd received initially from the nuclear medicine folks. My earlier confusion and fear were replaced with confidence and hope.

Okay... so let me paint you a picture to show you what was going on with my health. Cancer and friends: all manner of pathogens, bacteria, amoeba, and flukes had come to the party. Some were just arriving, whilst others were settling in and having a right ol' time. My abdominal area was particularly active in a super spreader sort of way – my pancreas, bowel, stomach, and liver were apparently akin to condomless pathogens gone wild at a free-for-all orgy with cancerous cells spreading rapidly in a thoroughly disorganized fashion. In other areas, my brain, lungs, and lymphatic system it was more like the State of the Union address the pathogens were moving in a painfully predictable and easy-to-miss sort of way. In addition to that, my toxicity levels were absurd, nearing the whole "incompatible with life" space. Big picture, things had gotten out of hand, and conventional wisdom held that I was kinda screwed. Thank God I wasn't buying into conventional wisdom.

Treatment protocols were designed and committed to. We were going to throw everything and the kitchen sink at this. But before that, my next stop was, of course, another adventure. This time I was off to the Amazon jungle.

My dear friend Yossi Ghinsberg and I met up in La Paz, Bolivia. Extraordinarily, a few years earlier, Yossi had gotten lost in the Amazon jungle and had survived for more than three weeks on his own with nothing but his mind, heart, and the clothes he wore. He was bound and determined that I should live and introduced me to both the jungle and the healers who'd played such instrumental parts in shaping his survival and his life. I really don't know how to convey the depth and breadth of my experiences in the Amazon. I probably don't ever want to know what I ate, drank, and had rubbed into my body. The things I saw and did range from the sublime to the ridiculous and the divine to the miraculous. It was… well… it was freakin' awesome as the proven healing effects of the Amazon and Pache-mama's mind-blowing cornucopia of herbs and potions coupled with the love and support of the people I met did what they were able to do.

All too soon, it was time for me to head back to Dr. Tom, my doctor of integrative medicine in New York. With his incredible team, he focused on finding and eliminating all the causes of my dysfunctions on all levels: biochemical and physical, mental, emotional, and spiritual. His goal was to help my body restore its natural healing ability and reestablish balance and harmony, which he knew would return me to complete health. To get us there, he would draw upon decades of experience, research, and discoveries in fields ranging from molecular biology, behavioral science, quantum physics, human consciousness, functional medicine, psychology, immunology, and many others. The blend of ancient healing arts, modern medicine, a vegan diet, and a whole lot of common sense coupled with a refreshing focus on being healthy versus being sick. All our attention and energy were focused on healing rather than dying and promised what I thought were miraculous results.

Once we'd discussed the results of the exhaustive and conclusive tests that Dr. Tom ran during my intake, we committed to never again naming nor discussing what had been wrong with me. That was in the past, and we were focusing on and working towards a healthy future. It was invigorating; with the exception of the two times when the outside world intruded, and Dr. Tom kindly wrote letters – one that was demanded by my wife's divorce attorney and the other required by the IRS — we were able to meet our commitment and focus exclusively upon me getting well. I dove headfirst into the many and varied treatment modalities aided by a hefty dose of applied neuroplasticity and epigenetics, love, prayers, good thoughts, and best wishes from family, friends, friends of friends, and so many people all around the world, most of whom I'll personally never meet. It came as no surprise to our team when a little more than a year after embarking upon my "Health-Scare Adventure", I'd seemingly gotten rid of everything that was killing me... the pathogens, amoeba, bacteria, flukes, and the adversarial life situation I was navigating were all gone, and I gratefully had a new lease on life. I'd been sick, and then I was well.

Unencumbered by the machinations of a dysfunctional life, I got a do-over. I got to build and live my life anew. I was single. I had three incredible children. I loved what I did to earn a living and appreciated the people I got to work with. I learned a lot about love, about loving myself and others, and how loving someone too much can be just as detrimental to a relationship as not loving them enough is. I was living, loving, learning, and muddling my way through life as best I could. My relationships with my children, whilst not always easy, were deepening and improving, as was my ability to function effectively, to take care of who and what I cared about in the world, both personally and professionally.

With all that said, as an objective observer might say, 2020 sucked for me right from the get-go. A relationship that'd meant a lot to me had ended unexpectedly. By March 2020, COVID-19 had arrived in my life, and as with everyone else on the planet, life changed. On June 28th, 2020, my fifteen-year-old daughter, Erin, had a seizure and died.

As I struggled to make sense of the world and be who I needed to be for my children and those others in my life who relied upon me and to who I was committed, I was grateful that I'd met someone who was willing and able to support me. With COVID-19 in play, we'd started as voices on a telephone. That someone was Rebecca. She lives in Chicago but is originally from Wisconsin. When we met, she was quarantined on her own at "The River House," a family home in the middle of nowhere Wisconsin. Our paths had crossed briefly and quickly diverged months earlier, and then, during COVID-19, we reconnected with one another. She was really easy to talk to, and our daily calls were a sanity saver as I navigated quarantined isolation from everyone and everything I'd known. She seemed to me to be everything I'm not... smart, sophisticated, humble, focused, disciplined, reliable, structured, and predictable. Though we were both decidedly single and not seriously searching for romantic coupling, we marveled at how well we got along whilst being precisely who and what neither of us was looking for.

One of Rebecca's solid red lines that she was adamant she would not cross when it came to considering potential suitors was tattoos. I have a lot of tattoos. Most relevant to this conversation, I was initially extremely pissed at God when Erin died. Rebecca has a graduate degree in Theology and works for God and worked for the Catholic Church. We got to talking about how almost every day I was with Erin, we'd go for walks, and we'd go through our tattooed prayer rotation. You see, each of my tattoos showed up during my "Health-Scare Adventure" and its aftermath; each has deep and profound meaning to me and, when strung together, create something akin to a rosary, a mala if you like, of insights, prayers, and reflections. Rebecca and I explored what the tattoos meant to me and what considering them revealed to her. We hope that reading and considering what we have to offer is of help to you.

Rebecca

"I didn't die!"

At midnight on January 1, 2020, I messaged my close friends and family to let them know that 2019 had not killed me! I had lived through the whole year! It was now officially 2020, and I hadn't died!

I stood dancing in sequin-covered, knee-high boots, excited, proud, and admittedly somewhat disbelieving that I had made it through 2019. No, I had neither been diagnosed with a terminal illness nor been in a plane crash. I hadn't even had an accident in the most dangerous room in the house. I hadn't done any of these things. What I had done was endure my second divorce.

As a result of the change in my relationship status, there were many moments during 2019 when I believed the devastation and sadness of my emotions were going to kill me. I felt that death was so close to befriending me that I removed my soon-to-be ex-spouse as the beneficiary on my retirement plan and life insurance policy within 36 hours of his announcement that he wanted a divorce. I had made a miscalculation, though, because here I was moments into 2020, fully alive with champagne in hand, realizing I hadn't died! Actually, I was nowhere near close to death. As it turns out, I was going through a sort of rebirth. It was a classic story of meta-morphous. Just when the caterpillar thought the world was over it became a sequin-covered butterfly.

About ten weeks after New Year's Eve, the Coronavirus was rapidly spreading through the US. With the arrival of COVID-19, a shelter in place order was put in effect for the city of Chicago (where I live), and all of my work moved from in-person to remote. So I left my condo in the sky for the land of my birth, Wisconsin. I packed my car full of clothing, work gear, and my SodaStream to drive north to where I grew up in rural Wisconsin. Considering more people were residing in my Chicago high-rise building than occupants in the town where I went to middle school, I figured my chances of coming into contact with COVID-19 would be much smaller there.

My early COVID-19 mantra was, "this is a lesson in adaptability." This was partly to remind me that you adapt (evolve) or die. Since I had lived through 2019, I was now quite determined to live through COVID-19. One area that the Coronavirus had forced me to adapt was the way I dated. It removed the standard potential partner preferences that I held in place during my typical vetting process: He should be well dressed, have good taste in and knowledge of restaurants, not live in the suburbs, and have no tattoos. Paul would automatically have been disqualified with a score of 0/4.

At this point, Paul and I had lived through divorce, diagnoses, and the distresses that life brings. These events have marked us both for life—Paul, literally with tattoos and scars. I had emotional pain and invisible wounds. Each of us has marks, scars, and wounds in our own way. Marks that shape who we become or don't become. Bigger than any of these scars, though, we have been marked as children of God. By God, we have been marked for life. Paul and I both know that life brings unfathomably challenging and painful moments. However, we believe that grace and grit can help get us through these excruciating moments. We hope you discover the grace around you and the grit within you to live as someone who has been marked for life.

Date: 04/29/2017 | Placement: Back. Right shoulder. | Art: Gabriel Wolffe from Hebrew Tattoos | Tattoo Artist: Aura Dalian | Elements: Hebrew "Thy will be done." (Atop) "Lord I believe." (Below) Hippo.

LORD, I BELIEVE. THY WILL BE DONE

Paul

Getting my first tattoo surprised a lot of people and was a lot easier to do than I'd have imagined it'd be.

It's kinda ironic as up 'till that point, when it came to anything to do with tattoos, whether asked for my opinion or not, I'd always been a pugnacious, "Don't do it. You'll regret it," kinda guy. I was a bit of a prude, looking down my nose at anyone who'd been inked with a distasteful "NQOCD" (Not Quite Our Class, Darling) flare of my nostril and ever so quiet cluck of my tongue. It doesn't matter that I was well-intentioned for the most part. I was an arrogant, narrow-minded SOB, convinced being inked was an unnecessary, self-imposed sentence to a life of being judged as *less than* by others, of placing unnecessary roadblocks upon your career path, and of years of regret as one grew old, fat, and wrinkly and the ink faded, and the artwork stretched grotesquely. Bottom line, I thought that getting a tattoo was a bad choice and that people who had tattoos were people who had a propensity for making bad choices.

The good thing about life is that we all have the opportunity to live and learn and change our minds about things. So often, things we see today as facts, tomorrow we may see as well-intentioned opinions.

Whenever I'm locked into a position with certainty, particularly when I'm seeing myself as being right and someone else as being wrong, I can see that by taking my position, I'm the one causing myself (or them) angst or unhappiness. I realize that all that angst and stress is optional. If I can step back and look at the situation (people getting tattoos, COVID-19, etc.) as it is, I can remind myself that the primary cause of most of the angst or unhappiness that I experience in my life is seldom due to whatever is going on. Rather, it is a result of my thoughts about the situation, and I can do something about it. When I'm able to see the situation with neutrality, I can see whatever value I choose to ascribe to it is the value that I'm choosing to ascribe. My opinion doesn't make my circumstance true or real. It just makes it true or real to me. By being able to see that and being willing to change, life stops being such a struggle and instead becomes a magnificent adventure, pregnant with opportunity and change. None of us have to be, or even could be if we wanted to be, exactly the same people today as yesterday. Thank goodness for that. Today, I really, really like my tattoos and am enthralled by others' art. I'm curious whenever I see anyone else's ink as I remind myself that every tattoo has a story and the canvas behind that art has a life and story too.

The inspiration for my first tattoo was of the "No shit, Sherlock," variety. I was in Israel and had just spent my day exploring Jerusalem. Given everything that was going on in my life at the time, some of the day had been spent on my knees, with my head bowed and eyes closed in prayer in the Church of the Holy Sepulchre. I was surprised at the blend of awe and reverence I felt, coupled with expressions of heartfelt gratitude and appreciation that spontaneously pulsated through my body before being punctuated by my lamenting, complaining, and questioning my lot in life. All of this was topped off with a hefty dollop of begging and bargaining. Quite a prayer cycle.

Other parts of my day I'd spent on my feet, a curious blend of awe and dread as I passed through the gates and trod the well-worn trails, including the path Jesus had walked on his last day in the flesh. Spoiler alert, I knew how that story ended. Sitting on my backside, overlooking the Mount of Olives and parts of Old Jerusalem, I got to thinking about the crosses and the hippos in our lives.

Now to be crystal clear, I'm not for one nanosecond comparing myself nor my experience on the Zambezi River with that pissed off hippo to JC's experience in Jerusalem or the days leading up to and including the day he was crucified. That said, sitting in that holy of holy places, not far from the gardens of Gethsemane, the parallels weren't lost on me between his life, my life, our deaths and transfigurations, and the life of every single person who has ever lived or whoever will live.

Shit happens. We get to choose what happens next.

Shit's always going to happen. It's inevitable. Life is a participation sport, and sometimes really bad things happen to really good people. Sometimes seemingly good things happen to bad people. I know I'm stating the obvious here; all the time, something is happening to everyone. The beautiful thing is that, knowingly or unknowingly, we get to choose what happens next. We get to choose how we respond — either by what we do or by what we fail to do.

Viktor Frankl, the renowned Austrian neurologist, psychiatrist, philosopher, author, and Holocaust survivor, came to mind while sitting under the blazing sun. I thought about how during some of his most harrowing experiences in Nazi Concentration Camps, he was presented with evidence time and time and time again that:

> *"When we are no longer able to change a situation, we are challenged to change ourselves.*
>
> *Everything can be taken from a man but one thing: the last of the human freedoms—to choose one's attitude in any given set of circumstances, to choose one's own way.*
>
> *Between stimulus and response, there is a space. In that space is our power to choose our response. In our response lies our growth and our freedom."*

Viktor and I were on the same page. Between shit happening (stimulus) and what happens next (response), there is a space – Eckard Tolle calls that space "Now." The Power of Now is that moment when we're truly present; we have authentic access to the power of choice and therein lies the opportunity for growth and the promise of agency, dignity, and freedom.

I was extremely grateful that Jesus had such deep faith and huge cajones. In that space, he made the choices that he made that night in the Garden of Gethsemane and, with it, bought me my freedom to choose how to live my life. Thanks, Jesus.

I thought about Viktor. I thought about Jesus. I thought about that hippo who'd ripped my body and my life apart, that hippo who'd killed the old me. I thought about how I'd lost my arm and my life as I knew it. I thought about the effect that had had on my life and so many other people's lives. Cognitively, I remembered the moment the realization sunk in that I couldn't change what had happened or the potential implications that had on my future. I remembered the overwhelming and thoroughly demoralizing and debilitating despair that had engulfed me.

And then... and then viscerally, my body shuddered as it recalled the moment it realized that I had the power to choose whatever happened next. That moment when I realized that from then on, my attitude, the words that came out of my mouth, and my actions, all of it, each and every element of it all of the time... that was going to be entirely up to me. Those were choices that I got to make on a choice-by-choice basis. I got to choose what happened next and had agency over how the rest of my life was going to unfold. Whilst losing my arm and everything that went with that sucked, realizing I possessed the power of choice rocked! The phoenix really did have the opportunity to rise up out of the ashes.

Albeit incredibly briefly, I was somewhat exhilarated for the first time in a long time. All too soon, of its own volition, my mind seemed to say to itself, *enough of that,* as it leapt from its happy place to my current situation. Exhilaration morphed into despair as I recalled how my health and my marriage were a three-lane shit show. Anger. Fear. Sadness. Hurt. Confusion. Overwhelm. My marriage was dying, and with it, the life and the family I loved were dying too. No real surprise that my body was following suit.

All sorts of neural pathways were lighting up the smarty pants in me (I'd recently invested in a company exploring the benefits of applied neuroplasticity) knew it was just neurons firing and a series of correlating thinking and feeling reactions. Almost instantaneously, I felt really shitty. I was trapped on that three-lane shit show neural highway hurtling towards the opportunity to make a lot of bad choices. Rational Paul had left the scene and his grumpy, ugly, alter ego had taken control. Let's just say anger, heroic suffering, overwhelm, and self-righteous indignation are not pretty colors for me.

Brief aside, it'll give you some insight into how my mind works as you join Rebecca and me on this adventure. I was born and raised in a Christian home, raised Catholic. I've explored and dabbled in more religions and spiritual traditions than I can currently name. Mystics, Shamans, poets, televangelists, survivors, barstool philosophers, and neuroscientists intrigue me. I believe that crystals are a thing. I kinda buy into my horoscope and am a fan of psychology, philosophy, and science. A voracious learner with (for the most part) an open mind, I believe that anything is possible and that gratitude, kindness, and love are superpowers that we all possess. We have the power to utilize them at will if we choose to.

I knew I didn't want to feel grumpy and waste the experience of being in Jerusalem nor mess it up for the people I was with. I took a breath, found the *space*, got present, and chose to do something. First, I thought about something I was grateful for; I pictured my three kids back home playing in the yard as clearly and with as much detail as I was able to. I pictured the smiles on their faces heard the sounds of their laughter. I let myself enjoy how that felt, the smile curling the corners of my mouth and warming up my heart. Before I knew it, grumpy had left the building, and grateful Paul was back. I'd just *scienced* myself.

Apparently, it's neurophysiologically impossible to be grateful and grumpy simultaneously. I had a lot to be grateful for, so I chose that rather than letting anger, fear, sadness, hurt, confusion, and overwhelm color the lens through which I saw my present and future. Somewhere *between stimulus and response* in that still small *space*, I'd allowed and chosen for different neurons to start firing and different neural pathways to light up. I chose to be grateful instead.

Sitting there overlooking Old Jerusalem, it shocked the bejesus out of me when out of a place of profound gratitude and appreciation, the next thoughts that arose in my mind and my body, the sounds that came out of my mouth, were, "Lord, I believe," and "Thy will be done." With those two short utterances, prayers if you will, declarations to the universe, I felt my body settle a little. I took a few deep breaths, and as my faith kicked in, I knew that everything was going to be alright. "Lord, I believe," and "Thy will be done," were my go-to declarations. I'd embodied them at very different times in my life and often used them interchangeably and, when I really needed to, used them together. This was a time I *really* needed to use them.

"Thy will be done,…" was an assimilation. It'd been years of indoctrination at my Catholic boarding school, a few near-death experiences wherein Divine intervention was one of the very few explanations that make any sense when it comes to explaining how I survived, coupled with a miraculous healing or two along the way.

Then there was the indisputable personal experience, the correlation between taking a few deep breaths, getting still, finding the *space,* choosing faith over fear, and saying the words: "Lord, I believe, thy will be done," and feeling the peace and acceptance that replace the fear and the uncertainty. I'm a simple man, and whilst I can't fully explain why putting my faith in God and declaring it so works. It just does. When shit happens, and I can get out of the way and trust God and have faith that things will work out the way that they're supposed to, I don't know how or why; if I leave them alone and keep doing the next right thing, they just seem to work out. They just do.

"Lord, I believe." I still smile every time I think about where this came from.

We were in the aftermath of the financial crisis of 2008. Cash was tight; consulting and speaking gigs were few and far between. It was the night before. I was pretty confident that a project I had been working on that provided my lifeblood was going to be canceled.

I'd flown in that evening and had been saying "Lord, I believe" on repeat, but I just wasn't feeling it. I tried it again and again. Nothing. Nothing at all. With a growing sense of dread and despair stalking me around my hotel room, something had me look up this televangelist chap who I listened to occasionally, Joel Osteen. I clicked a link… go figure, I interpreted his message of inspiration as a reminder that I needed to man up, get my head outta my arse, choose faith over fear, and remember that my faith and my expectancy lived hand in hand. He reminded me that God's got this and of one of JC's greatest hits, "Everything is possible for one who believes" (Mark 9:23). So, with his encouragement ringing in my ears and with an attitude of faith, I declared out loud, "Lord, I believe." I spent the rest of the evening believing and declaring, "Lord, I believe" and "Thy will be done." An air of expectancy replaced the prevailing sense of fear where I'd been living.

The next morning, I woke up, went to the meeting, and lost the contract. Trusting God had clearly been a mistake. "Shucks. What do I do now?" Walking through Baltimore airport in a daze a few hours later, I swung between "Lord, I believe" and "I'm screwed." I swung between faith and fear, I was already using my credit cards to pay my mortgage and some of my bills, and they were close to being maxed out. Income options seemed limited. Maybe I could sell some plasma. Nope, given my travel history, I wasn't even qualified to do that.

Waiting for my flight to board, with a conscious effort, I doubled down, "Lord, I believe," the prevailing message running through my mind on a loop. My phone rang. It was an international call from the UK. There was a consulting gig starting in London next week, was I interested? Traveling internationally was far from ideal when it came to being a dad and a husband. That said, it was the option I chose without hesitation over not paying my bills and supporting my family. Thanks, God. Thanks, Joel Osteen. Thanks, Máire – the person who I'd never met, who called me up on a whim as she needed a coach, and someone had told her they thought I could help. God's fingerprints were all over my salvation. "Lord, I believe – a lot."

So, a hippopotamus, "Thy will be done," and "Lord, I believe," in Hebrew calligraphy seemed the obvious choice for my first tattoo. I found the best tattoo artist I could find to do the ink work and contacted another artist whose work I loved to do the design.

Rebecca

For the vast majority of my life, I have not given hippos much thought. Clothing, boys, retirement plans, dinner reservations: these were the things that occupied my mind. I vaguely remember enjoying the game Hungry Hungry Hippos when I was younger. Even the Christmas song "I want a Hippopotamus for Christmas" was not interesting to me. I am more of a "Santa Baby" kind of girl wishing for a yacht or a '54 convertible. A hippo, no thanks. I'll pass. So, when Paul casually told me that he had been in a bad accident with a hippo while kayaking a river in

Africa, I was like, "WHAT!?!" I relayed the information to my brother, who apparently has kept his subscription to National Geographic current because his response was, "Hippos are the deadliest animals on the planet."

"They are!?"

Suffice it to say, after hearing Paul's story of the hippo attack, his survival, and what he did with his life afterward. Hippos have entered the forefront of my mind.

Coming off of my sudden divorce in 2019, survival was a prominent thought in my mind. Although I had no physical wounds to show anyone, I kept proclaiming, "But I didn't die!" to anyone within earshot. I felt as though I had just achieved a major victory. I had survived human emotions. My husband's departure had left me feeling like I should have been admitted to the emotional ICU. The onslaught of emotions that I experienced after his departure felt like they would be responsible for my death.

It wasn't that I wanted to die. I wasn't suicidal. I believed I had things to live for. It just seemed as though my feelings were going to kill me. It was akin to someone having an unexpected heart attack. They wanted to live. They were caught off guard. They were out getting a coffee and had more plans for their day, for their life. Suddenly, they experience severe chest pain, dizziness, and shortness of breath. The next thing they know, they are in the hospital. They want to live. They don't want this thing that is happening to their body to kill them, but it feels like it just might. That is how my emotions felt. They were attempting to squeeze the life out of me. As Paul and I got to know one another, he graciously listened and reassured me that severe emotional wounds can be just as fatal as rogue hippo attacks. In moments of wondering if I was going to make it through some of those days of 2019. I struggled to think, *"Lord, I believe,"* and *"Thy will be done."*

Theoretically, I am a fan of God's will. However, I am often tempted to believe that I know better. "Haha, funny girl," I can almost hear God saying. Like a small child who tells her mom that she is going to have $5 million saved up by the age of 10 because she has started saving her money in a piggy bank. Mom puts on a smile to humor the young girl, followed by, "Oh, that's great, honey." Knowing full well that her daughter will not save $5 million in the next four years of her life is potentially how God reacts to me, thinking I know better or more than God does.

Conversely, I have been able to believe with relative ease for the majority of my life. I did not always possess the language or the technical theological knowledge that I came to acquire later in my life, but I felt God. Sensing and being aware of the Divine had, for the most part, been an easy area of my life.

I don't necessarily have a traditional piety. I have a black and glittery gold chiffon scarf that says, "I ♥ Jesus." I have a t-shirt that reads, "Holy Chic." I have Jesus band-aids because obviously, Jesus heals. I have several other cheeky religious odds and ends that humor some and offend others. I don't have a rosary hanging from my review mirror. There are no icons or crosses displayed throughout my home. However, I have several quotes from saints and popes on one wall. These quotes hang mixed amongst Anne Lamott, Buddha, and Ani DiFranco quotations.

Following my second divorce, my faith went through a challenging phase. Challenging in the way that trying to lose weight after you're 40 isn't the same as it is in your 20's. I kept showing up at the gym. I kept trying to connect with God, but it wasn't working in the same way it had in the past. The trauma, the hurt, the pain, and the disbelief of what my life was stunted my faith. It interfered with my belief in God. It wasn't that I wouldn't eventually lose the weight or couldn't sometimes believe, but it felt like a lot of work. Decades ago, it had felt effortless.

Life can bring us to moments of unbelief. Moments of unbelief do not make up our totality. They are merely moments on our faith journey where it's harder to believe. At times God can feel far away or unknown. In the moments following my second divorce, I began to consider and believe in the power of evil and the devil in ways that I never had. God felt out of reach. My emotions had knocked me down. My faith wavered. My belief ebbed and flowed.

I knew enough not to go into the downward spiral of self-destruction by self-soothing with drugs, alcohol, etc. Yes, I would sometimes self-medicate with an abundance of donuts or cupcakes. I would tell myself it's just donuts, not heroin. I knew I was on an emotional precipice. I also knew that I couldn't ignore the feelings I was experiencing. I had to experience the horrific pain. I had to get through this desert to get to my promised land.

What brings people to faith is akin to asking what brings people to love one another. There isn't a formula that works for everyone. There isn't an instruction booklet of do X followed by Y, and you'll find the love of your life.

I don't think anyone with authentic genuine faith is constantly able to say with 100% conviction, "Lord, I believe." Similar to being in love. There are moments when you love someone, but you may not like them. For some reason, those warm, lovey feelings you had dissipated for a while. The same is true with lived faith. There are some moments of faith that you move through with unbelief, I learned to keep moving. "Don't stop," I'd tell myself. I allowed myself to go as slowly as I wanted or needed, but stopping was not allowed. I wanted my promised land, and I had an inkling that if I stopped in my desert of distress, I would die.

The Gospel of Mark gives us an insight into how God understands and what God expects around belief. The New International Version Bible (NIV) translation of Mark Chapter 9:23-24 reads:

> *"If you can?" said Jesus. "Everything is possible for one who believes." Immediately the boy's father exclaimed, I do believe; help me overcome my unbelief!"*

In this story, Jesus discloses two things to us. He lets us know that everything is possible for one who believes. It's as if Jesus is letting this father or man in on a secret. No registration is required. Without the need to enter a credit card or an email address, Jesus discloses the potency of belief. Jesus lets this man and us know how powerful belief is. Jesus doesn't ask the man to do anything, does not require the man to perform a task, and does not make the man answer any questions. Jesus merely offers insight into what belief can do.

Jesus does not command belief from this man but instead poses the question, "If you can?" The Jesus in Mark's gospel seems comfortable, allowing for a response of unbelief from the man (and us). Jesus doesn't say, "You must believe. You have to have faith. You have no other choice." Instead, Jesus invites man into the possibility of belief. In this verse, Jesus is asking the man "Is it possible for you to believe?" Jesus may be thinking, from where I am standing, it seems as though you are blocking yourself from believing. He is inviting the man to open the door to belief. Jesus knows that if the doorway to belief is cracked open, the possibilities that lie within that space will be made present.

Jesus' tactics work! The man immediately responds with, "Lord, I believe!" The man's response is not fake or lofty. He does not reply, "Oh, I love you so much, Lord! I have never loved anything more than I do you. My heart overflows with praise and adoration for you. From here forward, my life will be an outpouring of belief." No! He doesn't say anything like that. He admits that belief is hard, challenging, and sometimes his unbelief outweighs his belief. He reaches out and asks for help in his words, "I do believe; help me overcome my unbelief." Just like us, amidst his belief, he has unbelief. Jesus accepts that!

There was a stage in grieving for my marriage where I would spontaneously feel pain and cry. I was fearful of going to the store, parties, or anywhere that people would be confused by the sight of a sobbing woman. Attending church service was also hard for me. I wanted to feel closer to God. I knew attending Mass would help provide some familiarity and grounding for my fledgling faith. However, there were days when I wouldn't go, or I'd go to different churches for fear that my surprise sobbing would occur near someone I knew.

One Sunday, just as I was beginning to come around the first bend of my healing, the very beginning of, "Maybe, if I squint and think about it really hard, there might be a possibility that I will live through this," began to enter my brain. I went to my church, where I am an employee. I think it can be a bit awkward to show up at work and have an emotional meltdown. It was summer, so the programming I am typically in charge of was not happening. I got to be a regular person in the pews. I sat in the rear of the church.

I wore my long hair down. If I assumed the head bent in a prayer position, my hair would cover most of my face. At one point in the Mass, onlookers may have guessed that I was deep in prayer. The reality was that I was striking this pious pose to hide the water flowing from my eyes. I don't know what the readings were that day, but I do remember six words of the priest's homily, "The graces were to strengthen me."

I don't recall the story he told or what the graces in his homily were, but this concept cut right through me. I sobbed with relief. I went home.

I got out my dry erase marker and immediately wrote, "The graces were to STRENGTHEN me," on my bathroom mirror. They stared at me for months.

This perspective was comforting to me. If I had been given graces to strengthen me to prepare me for what I was enduring, then I would get through this situation that was currently my life. It just seemed too factual to not be true. If you intentionally take time to prepare for an upcoming presentation at your job, you will be ready. If each day you work on it, edit it, and diligently approach it by presentation day, you will be ready. On the other hand, if you binge-watch Netflix, go out with friends, avoid your presentation until the night before, chances are you will not be ready.

The phrase was eventually erased from my bathroom mirror and earned a permanent spot on my quote wall. One day while glancing at "The graces were to strengthen me," I had a collision of the words tattooed on Paul's body. "Thy will be done," and "Lord, I believe." While my life and belief didn't feel as certain as they had, I believed, and I was able to find strength in that belief to let God's will be done.

The concept of "Thy will be done" was something that I've grown into. I hear people confidently remark, "Let go and let God." Or "Jesus, take the wheel." No! I don't want to let go. I want to wrap my hands tightly around the wheel. I want to drive my route my way until my fingers are sore from squeezing the wheel so firmly! I often look at people who can easily take their hands off the wheel with confused admiration. They seem relaxed and likely have a lower heart rate than I do.

My ego and stubbornness have made me late to the "Thy will be done" game. It can sometimes be hard to trust and believe in something past our human understanding. Like fool's gold, a sort of confidence of *No, I know what to do. I know how this should go.* In my mind can seemingly usurp God's wisdom. It has been my experience that great things happen when I can get past this. I hear this in the stories of others and wonder how it is not taught in an *Essentials of Life* class somewhere. Life kept trying to teach me the lesson of letting God's will be done, but I was a resistant student.

Learning the lesson of letting God's will be done is hard, emotionally fraught, and scary. There is something that happens, though. Whether we call it God's will, manifesting, or trusting the universe, some shift occurs when we loosen our grip on the wheel.

Now when I think of hippos, I understand how dangerous and deadly they are. I suppose life itself is inevitably deadly. I realize my "survival" story is much more pedestrian than many. *Woman Gets Divorced* isn't newsworthy. It is a regular occurrence. In the US, there are over 750,000 divorces per year. It's likely that an overwhelming majority of people did not die as a result of the emotions that they experienced as a result of their divorce. Like the man in Mark's Gospel, I had belief mixed with unbelief, and that's okay. Belief is not a constant, and it may not be 100% certain. That seems acceptable to Jesus. I am, however, still 100% certain that I'd like a yacht rather than a hippopotamus for Christmas.

Date: 06/28/2017 | Placement: Inside right wrist. | Art: Gabriel
Wolffe from Hebrew Tattoos | Tattoo Artist: Pedro, Chicago
| Elements: Hebrew "Be, Then Do." Infinity sign.

BE, THEN DO

Paul

"How are you being whilst you're doing what you're doing?"

*The infinite possibilities born of being aware of who
I'm being whilst I'm doing what I'm doing.*

Sitting on a ledge overlooking the Mount of Olives in Jerusalem, I was struck by how small and insignificant I was. Yet, at the same time, I felt the infinite number of possibilities and opportunities at hand and the myriad of potential outcomes they held in my soul. Never before had feeling small and insignificant felt so good. Never before had the infinite number of opportunities, possibilities, or potential outcomes that lay ahead felt so friendly and accessible.

I was reveling in what I felt was my connection to the Divine as I spent this time in the Holy Land. My senses seemed hyper-activated as I sat beneath the burning Israeli sun and breathed in the dry desert air. The words *Be, then do* flooded my mind along with the absolute certainty that my path out of the illness-induced wilderness I was traversing was going to have less to do with what I did and more to do with who I was and how I was being whilst I did it. If I was going to be a jerk living out of fear and uncertainty, then my chances of seeing out the year were probably slim to zip. On the other hand, if I was going to be and spread love – to myself and to others – as kumbaya-esque as that sounds, the possibilities seemed infinite.

Sitting there, I felt the indelible imprint of God's love nurturing, comforting, and healing me whilst simultaneously kicking me in the arse and bidding me to drive on.

The thoughts that swirled around my mind and the feelings that shrieked their presence as they coursed through my body were unmistakable. This was an aspect of me and my life that I needed to work on if I really was going to choose to be healthy and well.

As was its want much of the time, my mind went to my children. The blurry images of them playing on their swings in the backyard in Michigan, the densely vegetated ravine serving as the idyllic backdrop as they interacted ever so easily with each other, came into focus. All three of them truly and wholeheartedly loved each other, that much a blind man could see. There was an unmistakable ease – born of love and acceptance that permeated their ways with each other.

I sighed out loud in dismay as I recognized myself coming into view, connected yet so very obviously apart. I knew how this particular scene played out.

I'd walk out to the swing-set to be with my kids, Kate, Erin, Jack, and our dog Charlie. To take advantage of the opportunities to connect with them, play with them, spend some time with them, have some fun, be the dad I thought I was and who I wanted to be. It was with dismay that I watched the all too familiar scene unfold in my mind's eye. Kate and Jack started goofing around and talking with me, vying for my attention, approval, engagement, and connection. Then my phone buzzed. My attention went to the work text that'd just arrived that Saturday morning and away from my beloved children. I assured myself it'd just take a minute, that I'd reply. That I'd take care of what needed to be taken care of, then I'd get back to and give my kids my undivided attention. I justified my actions in a nanosecond by blindly bullshitting myself that paying attention to the work text was really important. I was responding to it (working) for my kids' wellbeing, to provide for them.

After a few half-hearted attempts to re-engage with me, Kate and Jack, in the act of self-preservation, protectively withdrew. I'd obliviously and unwittingly been their teacher, and they'd unfortunately learned, at a far too tender age, that trying to interact and connect with someone who was demonstrably either unwilling or unable to reciprocate clearly hurt too much and wasn't worth the risk or the effort. The prudent move was to withdraw and protect themselves. They were learning that in the face of what they perceived – at worst as indifference, at best, as a jerk move and a lack of care –they could regulate the impact that had on them. That they could exert an itty-bitty degree of control on the situation, regulating how much they let people hurt them by meeting perceived indifference and lack of care with withdrawal. Before I left the text conversation, Kate and Jack left the swings. Erin and Charlie, the dog, remained behind to give me another chance.

My gut and solar plexus filled with dread as I recalled the event. I knew what was going to happen next. Erin had some profound special needs and was challenged when it came to communicating in a traditional linguistic fashion. That said, she had no problem communicating beautifully with anyone who wanted to connect with her.

As one of the loves of my life, she was a communicator par excellence when I took the time to connect, listen, and communicate with her. Initially, I communicated predominantly with my words, attention, actions, and body language. However, she masterfully communicated with me with her heart, presence, and eyes with love. With how she was, her being whilst she did whatever it was that she was doing.

Standing by the swings, feeling somewhat chagrined by Jack and Kate's departure, I was a little bristly as I tried to defend myself to Erin and Charlie.

"No one appreciates how hard I work or how much I have to do to keep everyone fed, clothed, and housed. Do you think I wouldn't love just to chill out and play?" I whined with an embarrassingly high level of pompous heroic suffering.

Charlie was just plain ol' embarrassed for me. He got up, shook himself off, without even a glance in my direction, trotted off to the back door and the relative peace indoors.

Erin hung in there a while longer. She smiled at me. The depths of light, love, and compassion in her eyes, coupled with the radiance and generosity of her smile, could warm even the most frozen and fractured of hearts. Had my phone not buzzed again at that precise moment, my recounting of the experience probably would have had a different ending. But my phone did buzz. My attention and my energy went from Erin to my phone.

To this day, I have no idea who was messaging me or what it was about. Yet, to this day, I can vividly remember how I felt as I looked up and attempted to reconnect. I saw and realized the desolation and the hurt in her eyes, and as I watched the quiver of her lip, I knew unequivocally that at that moment, I'd marked us both for life.

As I sit here writing about, reflecting upon, and sharing our experience with you, I'd like to say I'd do anything to have that moment back. A do-over, if you will. The truth is, I wouldn't if it meant I had to forgo the lessons I learned, the lessons that Kate, Jack, Erin, and Charlie taught me that day.

Often when I get sad, grumpy, or pissed off, my daughter Kate will ask me if I'm winning or if I'm learning. It's easy for me to poo-poo her question as some Pinterest-inspired-pop-psychology platitude.

Along the way, I've discovered that it's more useful to acknowledge that it's actually a trick question; that once I bring my attention to an event and/or experience, I'm actually doing both… winning and learning.

You see, on that day, I learned and won. I won if the game I'm playing – this life I'm living – is built around me intentionally taking care of who and what I care about. I win if – regardless of the circumstances – I like the answers that arise when I ask myself the question, *how am I being whilst I'm doing what I'm doing?*

And just like that, I was back at my vantage point, overlooking the Mount of Olives, and realized with a smile that I was being who I needed to be if I wanted to do what I needed to do, which included sticking around for a while for my kids' sake.

Rebecca

Why is it so hard to figure out who you are?! Shouldn't this be an easy endeavor? You're you. Literally, you are the only one of you – there is no other you (Taylor Swift said so). Yet, it seems so challenging to embrace ourselves. How fantastic is it that we are each wonderfully and uniquely made by God, yet how maddening it is that we are different and unique? Who amongst us hasn't pondered their purpose in life? Ironically, we spend a lot of money and time using our actual lives to figure out what we should be doing with our lives. Why are we struggling to solve this dilemma like a high school student in the 1990's trying to solve an equation using common core math? There are countless books and assessments on the topic, life coaches, retreats, gurus, and groups attempting to help people determine their purpose and who they are. Why can't this be easy, like ordering something with Amazon Prime? Can't we just automatically get a Prime life delivered to our door?

Each of us has been created for a life that is uniquely ours. God has gifted us with a distinctive life that is solely ours. Each of us has a unique and special purpose for being, a purpose that cannot be replicated or mimicked, and one that has not occurred and will never occur again. This time, this life is uniquely ours to live and step into. It's up to us to live the life God has gifted us with and not squander the possibilities that unfold before us.

When I first saw this tattoo, it didn't register to me as an infinity symbol. To me, it looked like a track. Had I just failed some Rorschach tattoo test? Knowing the words were "Be, then do." The thought, "Ugh!" came to mind. Be, then do, be, then do, be, then do, be, then do, be, then do, be, then do, be, then do, be, then do, be, then do, be, then do, that's exhausting. I did not want to be reminded by this design on the inside of Paul's wrist that I was to be, then do. There are enough deadlines at work, home projects, kids to take care of, groceries to buy, an endless battle with dust that just keeps coming and attaching itself to furniture, holidays to get through, and the list goes on and on just like the infinity track went on and on when I first saw it.

Time passed, and I let this tattoo grow familiar to my eyes and brain. The image of the infinity symbol with the words "Be, then do" started to become a wonderful reminder to me. Instead of seeing it as an exhausting track, I began to see it as an ongoing invitation to become my authentic self. Even though it was on Paul's body, I was a daily viewer of this symbol. It was almost as if God had gifted me with its placement on his wrist to remind me that the work of creating *me* was not finished.

For me, one of the positive outcomes of COVID-19 was the opportunity to reconnect with myself. I was not concerned about what others were doing, wearing, or how they were *being*. I was reminded that not even during a pandemic do I want to bake bread. However, I want to wear high heels and have a cocktail on a Friday night at my very exclusive home bar where no one but the resident is allowed entry. I got back to partnering with God and reclaiming and creating who I am.

The journey of becoming one's authentic self is continual. There is not a finite moment of point where we stop becoming. We are constantly growing and evolving our authentic selves. God is constantly beckoning us to become. With each day of our life who we are is continually being created. In the decisions we make, the actions we take, and the things we do and think, we become co-creators with God. God is always doing God's part, but the unfortunate reality is that sometimes we become complacent co-creators.

Holding the words "Be, then do" simultaneously with the infinity symbol finally made sense to my eyes and brain! It made even more sense when I thought back to high school math and remembered that infinity is actually understood as never being reached. It is counted towards infinite numbers but does not have a finite end point. Just like the infinity symbol (∞) is a sign that indicates constant growth and progress toward infinity. We, too, are constantly getting closer to our authentic selves while we are ourselves. This may be just as challenging as solving a quadratic equation, but this is good news!

The way I am me will be different from how you are you. We are going to be different from every other person. If you haven't already, start to become aware of how you react to what you do with your day and life. Become aware of your internal murmurs. There are times when our insides scream. When your feelings so obviously gnaw at you like a new puppy will feverishly gnaw its way through your favorite pair of shoes. We know that those are situations that we should not be in. Those are not the moments that we have to learn to attune ourselves to.

Most moments of knowing who we are are small murmurs; some are slightly uncomfortable, some are painful, and others are somewhat doubtful. On the other hand, murmurs may feel light, freeing, and smile-inducing. Start to realize what's making you feel these things. Just because so-and-so says having seven kids makes her happy doesn't mean that it's going to make you happy. Just because so-and-so loves to travel doesn't mean that being a homebody isn't what you're meant to be. Start becoming aware of your murmurs. Start going steady with your murmurs, begin to listen to them, and respond to them. Remember, this is an exclusive relationship, don't follow someone else's murmurs.

Once you learn to attune yourself to your murmurs, then take the next step – listen to them. There may be some that show up that you don't like. If you want to learn to be yourself, you cannot treat the murmurs you don't want to listen to like a bad song on a playlist. You cannot just skip the ones you don't want to hear. Pay attention to all of them, even if they don't fit your plan or feel uncomfortable, even if they challenge or scare you. You're learning to be yourself. This is no easy task, but you are awesome, so it will be worth it. After becoming aware of these little nudges that are trying to whisper hints about you, to you, start to listen to them. Really listen to them! Which ones are repeatedly showing up in your body, on your heart, or in your mind?

The being will become a bit more familiar, and once you make progress, you will find that you aren't done. Remember, you have been gifted, an infinite loop of becoming who you are. Sometimes it's going to be difficult, and sometimes it will be exhausting, but if you keep at it, it's going to pay off.

One of the most beautiful things about *doing* is that others get to experience you as a gift in their life. God gifting each of us with a unique life is also a gift to others. I have found that when I encounter authentic people, I learn and grow as a result of hearing their stories, and knowing them. The gift of who they are spreads out much like a shared flame can spread light far beyond its original source. The *doing* that comes out of authentically *being* is sacred, and in my experience, it is exponentially beneficial for those who encounter it in others.

Mark Twain wrote, "The two most important days in your life are the day you are born, and the day you find out why." Living our true life is a gift to God, ourselves, and others around us. Hiding ourselves, being uncomfortable, or hating parts of ourselves squander God's gift to us. We are made in the image and likeness of God. That in and of itself is worthy of celebration! A Divine spark dwells within us, and God calls each of us to go and do, to ignite the world with our special light.

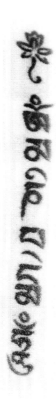

Date: 07/21/2017 | Placement: Left ribs. | Tattoo Artist: Amanda.
| Elements: Tibetan script. Om mani padme hum.

OM MANI PADME HUM

Paul

Not being able to settle on whether I was going to live or die, I leaned towards living. That said, I wasn't really sure how I was going to pull it off. But I was clear that if I was going to live, I needed to make some money. I had bills to pay and children to take care of, including their financial needs. Added to that, all this searching the globe for alternate healing was expensive.

In part, I'd been drawn to Nepal by the allure of climbing through the Himalayas and, in particular, Mount Everest. In addition to climbing, I was there chasing down a business opportunity. We were shooting footage for a pilot reality television series that I was potentially going to host. At the time, I was desperate to find something to believe in and anything that would give me a reason to live beyond loving my kids.

The show had been pitched to me in such a way that I couldn't say no. Travel the world and interview people, who, like me, had survived extreme situations and who, through their adversity, had gained some credible insights. They'd been able to articulate, embody, apply, and share those insights and were now living life more purposefully and happily. These people were making the world a better place by helping others. We thought that audiences would be interested in their real stories and the stories behind and beyond those that are so often shared by the media and well-intentioned PR firms.

The heady blend of real deal entertainment, extreme adventure, philanthropy, humor, learning, inspiration, motivation, and exotic locales really appealed to me. I also hoped that opportunities would find me to expand the footprint of my own 501(C)3 non-profit, Templer Foundation. I was confident I'd cross paths with someone along the way who'd touch my heart and inspire me to invest in them and their future. I may have been struggling financially, but I still felt incredibly drawn toward supporting worthy causes that aligned with our mission. Maybe it was God directing me, or perhaps it had something to do with whatever was going on inside my stricken brain.

Adventure, business development, and philanthropy are three of my favorite things. Throw in the possibility of rubbing shoulders and deep-dive conversations with the many Buddhists I'd inevitably encounter in Nepal; the possibility of even a modicum of enlightenment, healing for my body, and peace for my soul was extremely seductive, and I was all in.

Gary Guller, an extreme survivor and the first person without an arm to summit Mount Everest (before doing a lot of other very cool philanthropic stuff, including founding his Make Others Greater Foundation), was our subject and we met in Nepal, home to Kathmandu, the Himalayas, and Mount Everest.

Before heading off to the Himalayas and Mount Everest, Gary had arranged an audience with and a blessing from the Karmapa Lama for the entire crew.

When invited to ask any questions, I quoted a section of Seng-ts'an's (the Third Patriarch of Zen) Hsin-hsin Ming: *Verses on the Faith – Mind* and shared how I was struggling with it.

> *"The Great Way is not difficult for those not attached to preferences. When neither like nor dislike arises, all is clear and undisguised. If you wish to know the truth, then hold to no opinions for or against anything. To set up what you like against what you dislike is the dis-ease of the mind."*

As the conversation unfolded, I clearly saw that I had so many preferences to which I was very attached. At one end of the spectrum, I wanted to stay alive, be at peace, and be a part of a healthy, happy family. My most elusive vanity preferences were six-pack abs, two arms, and perfect teeth on the other end. I wished smoking didn't kill nor smell so bad, fast-food was good for me, that alcohol was my friend, and that relationships were easy.

As I dropped a little deeper into the conversation, I realized that I was bouncing between options with everything I was experiencing. Option A: A strong, ambitious preference to live in blissful acceptance of everything as it was whilst simultaneously building a future worth living for, and Option B: A strong preference for it all to be over and done. I was tired and had gotten to the point where, whilst in no rush to get there, I was ready to meet God if, as I believed, He/She/It was real. If I was wrong, I was ready for it all just to be over.

In moments when I could be honest with myself, I was getting so very tired of it all. My marriage was dissolving when I didn't want it to, and the impact it was having on my kids was absolutely devastating. Being ill sucked too. I didn't want things to go the way they were going, and I couldn't see any way to stop them. I knew what I wanted, and I wanted it now. Stop the madness. If you're real God, please stop the madness, please!

By letting myself, or rather, by choosing to be attached to all these preferences, I was totally stressed out and experiencing my life in ways that I wasn't committed to continuing.

Ironically the manifestation of my choices didn't just show up as me being an uptight jerk making others miserable along the way. It was quite literally killing me too. I was becoming quite well versed in the medical conversations regarding the many corollaries between what I was thinking and what was going on in my body and my life.

A term, psychophysiological coherence, lines up with Seng-ts'an's treatise. This occurs when our psychological (mental and emotional) and physiological (bodily) processes get in sync, and we experience greater emotional stability, have increased mental clarity, and improved cognitive function. In other words, when we're coherent, our body and brain work better, we feel better, and we perform better. Not to be glib but when unattached to our preferences and being coherent, life is more often than not – regardless of whatever is going on around you – pretty good.

On the other side of the coin, when we're attached to preferences and as incoherent as I was, everything seems to fall apart, opening the way for the shit to well and truly hit the fan. That's when another term that I'd become familiar with became more relevant, psychoneuroimmunology, the field of study that looks at the effect of our minds on our health and our disease resistance. By being an uptight jerk, I was hammering my immune system. In fact, I was pretty close to being the poster boy for having a ridiculously high allostatic load. Allostatic loads are the wear and tear on the body which accumulates as an individual is exposed to repeated or chronic stress.

With everything I was learning, I knew beyond a shadow of a doubt that if I didn't get my shit together, I was probably going to die sooner rather than later, and my kids would suffer unnecessarily. Vain as ever, I knew that I'd die with a paunch, and of all the things I had to worry about, that really pissed me off. It turns out that the stress hormone cortisol is also a major contributor to belly fat, so if I didn't figure out a way to de-stress, I'd have no shot at six-pack abs.

I digress; the short version of a long story is that spending some time with the Karmapa Lama is one of the most cherished experiences of my life to date. His kindness, wisdom, humility, power, and humor are unlike anything I've ever had the pleasure or the privilege to experience with anyone else.

I told him that I struggled with my attachment to preferences and asked for his help. He smiled gently, kindly, and insightfully – went exploring with me. We looked at my perceptions and perspectives as I showed him how I saw my life, health, relationships, past, and future. I showed him how I was navigating and moving through it all, and after a while – I paraphrase – he smiled and asked me how that was working for me. "Not so well." I teared up, and then we both smiled.

With his blessing, we headed off to the Himalayas. We had a lot going on.

Trekking through the Himalayas with Gary, Kim (the show's executive producer, my dear friend, and philanthropic partner in crime), the film crew, and our merry band of Sherpas, delivering school supplies to children in remote villages gave me lots of time to think, pray, listen, and learn. I engaged newly with myself and other people, which left me in no doubt that God's fingerprints were all over this leg of my adventure.

One of my most cherished memories from that chapter came after scaling a narrow path up a mountainside. I was leaning against a smaller rock next to another larger rock with the mantra *Om Mani Padme Hum* etched on it. Traipsing through the Himalayas, I'd seen the mantra etched onto rocks all over the place.

According to the Dalai Lama, Om Mani Padme Hum has the power to "transform your impure body, speech, and mind into the pure body, speech, and mind of a Buddha." I was told that if I focused on and repeated the mantra over and over again, I could raise the loving and unconditional qualities of compassion. Given my desire to lower my allostatic load by de-stressing, that seemed pretty cool and well worth exploring.

I asked for the literal meaning and context of the mantra. I was told it meant "Praise to the jewel in the lotus" and how all the teachings of Buddha are wrapped up in this one phrase. Seeing that I was confused, the Sherpa kindly explained to me that the lotus flower is within each of us, covered up by a lot of mud and muck. If we recite this mantra over and over again, with the right intention, we can get rid of the mud and muck until we are as sparkling, pure, compassionate, and wise as the lotus flower itself. I was getting a little closer to making sense of things.

As I traipsed through the mountains, I asked many questions about the mantra. It turns out that there are a lot of different meanings and different opinions on what each syllable in the mantra means. However, it is generally accepted that each syllable represents healing or purifying, something that doesn't work so well for us whilst bringing forth positive qualities.

So broken down, Om Mani Padme Hum can mean:

Om = lose pride and ego and gain kindness and generosity

Ma = lose jealousy and fleeting pleasures and gain ethical behavior

Ni = lose desire and passion and gain patience with ourselves and others

Pad = lose ignorance, prejudice, and judgment and gain diligence and perseverance

Me = lose attachment and possessiveness and gain concentration

Hum = lose aggression and hatred and gain unity, wisdom, and peace (coherence)

Also, apparently, when we chant *Om Mani Padme Hum,* it soothes the senses and sends energy to the parts of our body (or the chakra centers) that need it most. Nowadays, all sorts of medical folks acknowledge and agree that calming sounds (vibrations) help heal the body and mind.

I asked Nima Dawa Sherpa, a man I adored and respected the bejesus out of, if he thought reciting the mantra could help me connect with the kinder and more compassionate aspects of my character, aspects that had become somewhat jaded and inaccessible towards certain people in my life of late? In somewhat broken English, without pausing to consider, he offered (and I paraphrase) that choosing to be how I was and doing the things I was doing, I was obviously choosing to hurt myself. If I really did want to get well, I might want to get over myself. He went on to invite me to consider the reality newly that stuff's always going to happen. That if I'd just quit feeding my ego, feeling sorry for myself, and doing the whole heroic suffering thing, being so self-righteous and let go of my attachment to my preferences, to my need to be right, and have things be and go my way all the time, I might just find more peace and joy. He humorously suggested that I might even stop being the jerk I seemed to be so convinced everyone else was.

When we got to where we'd be sleeping that night, my thoughts were dragged from the abstract, philosophical, and spiritual realm and into the here and now. The weather had turned nasty, making the passes even more treacherous than usual, and removing leeches from our bodies wasn't getting any easier. We were gaining altitude, and one of our camera crew was really suffering from altitude sickness. As if that wasn't bad enough, all of our bodies were either swelling up, breaking down, or falling apart. Everyone had a case of ring sting and the screaming poops. That said, we were, for the most part, in pretty good spirits as we settled in for the night. Right up 'till the tiger showed up. Then there was much drama, yaks bleating, a tiger roaring, fires flaring, and Sherpas yelling.

We identified the main source of the drama. By now, the tiger was seemingly long gone, and there was a bigger problem at hand. The problem with tying livestock together to prevent one of them from being dragged off by a tiger is if one gets spooked and jumps off the side of a mountain, that doesn't necessarily work so well for his pals. Fear is contagious, and sudden panicked movements in times of stress, more often than not, are extremely hazardous – ask the yaks who were tied together hanging off the side of a mountain that night or the Sherpas who spent much of the night trying to sort things out. Hmmmm, maybe I should reconsider who I was tying myself to and recommit to no sudden movements when feeling really stressed?

All's well that ended well that night. All livestock were saved, and none of us were eaten by the tiger.

Unfortunately, though, the weather continued deteriorating, and the rest of our trip became more about survival and introspection and less about playing around and having fun. The trip took a particularly tragic turn when the plane we intended to use to get to Lukla crashed into the mountainside, killing both pilots. Then one of the people we were waiting for a helicopter medivac with died, too.

So, when I look at my tattoo, it reminds me that it is within myself to soothe and heal myself and that it's me who gets to choose which (if any) preferences I'm going to choose to be attached to. It's also an emphatic reminder that if I'm responsible and willing to do what I can do, stress and suffering are optional.

I have a pretty good idea of where much of my suffering originates. In my experience and understanding, if I don't tie myself to those people, places, things, or thoughts...or do or say harmful things... and focus instead on being grateful, being kind, and doing the next right thing, then I don't seem to suffer.

Rebecca

The New Testament is written in a dead language, Koine Greek. Dead languages aren't languages you can pick up through immersion or be exposed to through travel. Really the only way to learn languages like Latin, Koine Greek, or Sanskrit is by studying them. In grad school, I took a Koine Greek class. During this class, I learned that translating texts into different and living languages is no small feat.

The New Testament as we know it has chapters and verses, punctuation, and some printed versions even have the words of Jesus in red. The original Greek manuscripts were without punctuation. They did not contain numbers to indicate the division of chapters or verses and were only written in black or dark ink. To complete my homework and translate the Koine Greek text into English, I had to learn different voices, tenses, and sometimes how to translate the intent of the text rather than translate the text or word literally. There were a number of aspects to juggle while translating Greek into 21st century English. The good news was that my professor allowed us to write out the words of Jesus in whatever color ink we wanted!

In discovering that Paul had Om mani padme hum tattooed on his left ribs, the challenges of translation rushed back to me. I was unfamiliar with this Buddhist mantra inked on his body. I wanted to know what it meant. I quickly learned that I shouldn't be stuck on the literal translation of these six syllables, but on the intent of the mantra. I've learned that when literally translated into English, Om mani padme hum means "The jewel is in the lotus," or "Praise to the jewel in the lotus."

I approached this important Buddhist mantra as a student. I have an understanding of its intent and deep respect for all that the phrase brings to those who practice Buddhism. I have had the opportunity to know and chant with some Buddhist monks as well as visit a handful of Buddhist temples, but my experience and knowledge of Buddhism are limited.

I know that "Nostra Aetate" or "The Declaration on the Relation of the Church to Non-Christian Religions," written by Pope Paul VI in 1965, addresses the relationship and acceptance of Buddhism by Catholicism. In this declaration, Pope Paul VI writes:

> "Buddhism, in its various forms, realizes the radical insufficiency of this changeable world; it teaches a way by which men, in a devout and confident spirit, may be able either to acquire the state of perfect liberation or attain, by their own efforts or through higher help, supreme illumination…..The Catholic Church rejects nothing that is true and holy in these religions" (Nostra Aetate).

While I wouldn't be averse to finding a literal jewel inside each lotus flower, it is best to understand the intent and meaning of Om mani padme hum rather than its literal translation to the English language. Unlike the crops that grow in the fields of central Wisconsin, lotus flowers grow out of the mud. The leaves and flowers of the lotus rest upon the water, but its roots are buried and attached to mud. Mud is messy, wet, and in chillier temperatures, cold. It often attaches itself to things easily. Whether it is a pair of boots or a car that has driven down a muddy dirt road, some effort and elbow grease has to go into removing the mud from those surfaces. The lotus flower grows out of muddy water. It grows into a beautiful flower without a trace of mud on its petals once it appears above the water's surface. The lotus flower doesn't appear mud-less just once, but each evening it retreats into the water towards its muddy roots and re-emerges pristine and in bloom each day. The petals of the lotus routinely move down and into the mud, through water, and into the open air above the water's surface.

The intent, not the literal translation of Om mani padme hum, helps us to recognize the daily rhythm of rebirth. No matter how muddy or dark things have been we, like the lotus flower have a daily opportunity to bloom.

Our minds may want to hold onto the past, our errors, failings, and even our successes. Still, the lesson of the lotus flower encourages us to experience continual transformation and rebirth. A valuable and important lesson is made apparent through the natural cycle of the lotus flower. We are prompted to recognize that we have the opportunity to be transformed each and every day. No matter what the preceding day or year was like, we have the ability to shed the dirt and the mud that covered us and bloom into our beautiful selves.

Date: 09/16/2017 and 03/22/19 | Placement: Left stomach/waist. |
Tattoo Artist: Amanda. 09/16/2017 | Tattoo Artist: Aura Dalian
03/22/2019 | Elements: AMDG. Enso. Tree of Life. Yin-Yang. Rose.

CACOPHONY

Paul

I n September 2017, my day-to-day experience of life was not good. I was sick, sad, and scared. Confusion reigned, partly due to everything going on in my brain and partly due to everything going on in my life. I was grasping at straws, anything that would keep me afloat. The tattoo I started on September 16th, 2017, reminds me of how the world looked to me back then and is a roadmap of sorts that helps me navigate whatever life throws at me today.

I needed to dig deep, and one of the places I found comfort and refuge was in my past. From 1981 to 1986, I went to Saint George's College, a Catholic boarding school. It was run by an order of priests called the Jesuits. Their motto, Ad Majorem Dei Gloriam (AMDG), is the first element of the tattoo, and it translates into "For the greater glory of God." The message was drummed into us from day one at the school. The full phrase, attributed to Saint Ignatius Loyola, the founder of the Jesuit order, was actually Ad maiorem Dei Gloriam Inque Hominum Salutem," which loosely translates into "For the greater glory of God and the good of all humanity." Day in and day out – to the extent that we even wrote the acronym AMDG at the top of every page we wrote on. We were reminded that we had the pleasure and the privilege of being on planet Earth for the greater glory of God and the good of all humanity. I can't speak for all my schoolmates, but I think it'd be fair to say that most of us, even if it was begrudgingly believed it to be an element of our vocation and has influenced our careers and our paths in life.

I needed to constantly remind myself that no matter how sick, sad, and scared I was, I was still a beloved child of God and my reason for being was to find ways to live my life for the greater glory of God and for the good of all humanity. This was challenging on most days and nigh on freakin' impossible on others. But, at the same time, it gave me something to aspire to beyond my immediate circumstance.

Inside of my Ad Majorem Dei Gloriam tattoo, there is a circle, an enso. The one I have is drawn open, incomplete by design, and representative of the perfect imperfection of all things. It's related to the Zen idea of wabi-sabi, centered on accepting transience and imperfection, appreciating the beauty that is imperfect, impermanent, and incomplete in its very nature.

What drew me to the enso were the many and varied parallels it held to my life.

Being a physical and emotional amputee, having had my arm ripped off by a pissed-off hippopotamus, having had my wife unilaterally end our relationship, which simultaneously and irrevocably altered my relationships with my children, had the asymmetry and irregularity that the enso in part represents. With the most important relationships in my life torn asunder, the only way I could see to keep living my life was to reduce it to the simplest and most basic elements I could imagine. I'd been physically and emotionally beaten to within an inch of my life, and I was hoping that I'd somehow or another weather the storm. Instead, the experiences forced me to confront many of my iniquities and left me exposed without the energy or inclination for any pretense.

It wasn't all bad, though; there's the cliché that what doesn't kill you makes you stronger. I'm not one hundred percent convinced that's true. Whilst the pain and humiliation had been and continues to be fairly cathartic, imbuing a naturally subtle yet profound level of grace, freedom, and tranquility that I probably would never have been able to access, there are parts of me that would far rather have skipped those enlightening and strengthening experiences.

Inside of the enso is the yin-yang symbol. At the time, nothing seemed certain or to even make sense anymore. Yin-Yang was at play. There appeared to be a duality to everything. I looked at what was going on in my life: I was dying, and it was forcing me to live. My illness had become the catalyst for a profound commitment to health. As I knew them, my marriage and family life were ending, and a new life was beginning. Nothing it seemed was as it appeared. People, places, activities, relationships, and things that up until recently had seemed critical and essential, now seemed trivial and vice-versa. It could have driven me crazy but instead, embracing the duality of everything became extremely liberating. Nothing was inherently good or bad, right or wrong. Everything was interconnected in some way or another.

Inside the yin-yang symbol is a tree of life. The inspiration for the tree of life in my tattoo was a blend of biblical, practical, and spiritual influences. On the biblical side of the fence, I was drawn to the many references in "the Good Book," of how the tree of life represents the possibility of restoration of the life-giving presence of God after we've messed up. How if I seek it, I can find forgiveness for my sins and the promises of healing and resurrection through JC's sacrifice on the cross.

On the practical side, the tree of life symbol has its roots spreading down into the ground and its branches spreading upwards and outwards into the sky. This represents the interconnected nature and reliance of everything upon everything else. We're intrinsically connected to Pachamama (Mother Earth) and dependent upon her to grow and flourish.

This tied up nicely with the ancient symbolism associated with the tree of life, representing the uniqueness of each of our journeys, the need for physical and spiritual nourishment, and the inevitability of transformation.

The final element of the tattoo is a red rose inside of the tree of life that signifies love. When all else fails, as the Beatles told us, "All you need is love."

Rebecca

When someone is confirmed a Catholic, they can select a confirmation name. At the time of my confirmation, I proudly and intentionally chose St. Ignatius of Loyola as my confirmation name. I imagine that if someone had asked the Spanish soldier and eventual knight if he would have any impact on a teenage girl living in rural Wisconsin, Ignatius of Loyola would have probably said, "No." But about 500 years following his death, his life gives mine (and many others) some direction.

The small Catholic parish I grew up attending didn't have a vibrant youth group, children's choir, cry room, or anything specifically for kids. We went to Mass with the adults and were expected to sit, kneel upright (without our butt touching the edge of the pews), and stand with the adults. We also, like the adults, looked to the bulletin for more information about events or happenings. The year of my confirmation, I happened to read a stock bulletin article about discovering God with all five senses. I was enamored with the idea of smelling, tasting, touching, hearing, and seeing God. The article introduced me to Jesuit spirituality and St. Ignatius of Loyola. Ignatius was a Spaniard who was injured by a cannonball during a battle. As a result of his injury, he had some time on his hands to learn about God. Following his recovery, he devoted his life to God, founded the religious order of the Jesuits, and was eventually canonized as a saint by Pope Gregory XV.

Aside from thinking that my emotions were going to kill me, I haven't come anywhere close to actually being killed. Paul has come close to death numerous times. He has had last rites three times! No one has ever offered me last rites! He and Ignatius of Loyola encountered some terrible moments that left them both severely wounded and laid up in a hospital bed. Unlike the two of them, I have never had to spend one night in a hospital bed. I don't know if St. Ignatius was offered last rites after suffering a severe injury to both legs from a cannonball, but from reports of his earlier life, it sounds like he might have needed them. It seemed that sinning wasn't an occasional but was a regular occurrence for him. He was known to be quite the womanizer, had spent time in prison, enjoyed drinking and dancing into the night (okay, we did have that in common). The man who would someday be named a saint didn't shy away from "taking things outside" if tempers flared and a fight was needed. He was far from humble and concerned more about himself than others. Throughout his younger years, he sought power, prestige, and wealth. Yet, this man became one of the great saints of the Church. In his autobiography, he wrote of himself that he was extremely interested in having fame and concerned with the vanities of the world as a young man. This doesn't exactly sound saintly.

At the age of 30, all of these sinful interests surprisingly came to end for Ignatius. He was injured in a battle. While healing from an encounter with a cannonball, he had a lot of time on his hands. It is said that while he was laid up, there were only two books available for him to read. A thought that probably is unfathomable to us with our Kindles, iPads, audible, libraries, and more. He only had two choices: 1. Sit and do nothing, or 2. Pass the time by reading either about the life of Christ or the lives of the saints. It turns out he read both options and, as a result, was forever changed.

As a result of reading about Jesus and the saints, Ignatius changed. Once he was healed, he traveled to northern Spain. There he confessed his sins and began to live out his interior conversion. Leaving women, fighting, fame-seeking, and general soldier behavior behind, he instead sought out God and holy things. He became an ordained priest and eventually established the Society of Jesus, or as it is more commonly referred to, the Jesuit religious order, and was canonized a saint by Pope Gregory XV.

Ignatius of Loyola, whom I am sure many of us can relate to in one way or another (except for the cannonball incident) chose, "For the greater glory of God," as the motto of his religious order. This motto is tattooed in Latin "Ad Majorem Dei Gloriam" on Paul's torso.

I love a motto, a walk-up song, or a theme! My nickname in my college sorority was "Motto Mamma" because I was so taken with and would not stop infusing the sorority's motto into my daily conversations. The motto of the Jesuits reminds us that all we do and are working towards is "For the greater glory of God." We can get lost and consumed by thousands of different things, making money, being a good parent, being accepted, losing weight, and more. Yet, if we paused in the moments of our work, parenting, and search for ourselves and instead re-centered ourselves around "For the greater glory of God." I think we would find that it changed our orientation and attitude.

I have no intention of finding out, but I have to imagine it would make me feel courageous, accepted, and strong to have "For the greater glory of God" tattooed on me. As beloved children of God, we have been created for the greater glory of God. Each of us is uniquely and wonderfully made to help bring about the glory of God in our own particular way. Intellectually I know this, and it's one of the things I love about Christianity.

However, it's quite easy to let that get buried under the onslaught of stuff that life continually catapults at us. That's where "Ad Majorem Dei Gloriam" shows up and reminds us that we are meant to live a life that generates glory!

Mingled with the, "For the greater glory of God," text of this tattoo is the image of the tree of life. A tree of life shows up across numerous cultures and religions, and the concept spans thousands of years. The idea and image of a tree of life are present in the writings of the Mesopotamians, Native Americans, Buddhists, Muslims, Jews, and Christians.

At World Youth Day (an enormous Catholic gathering) in 2006, Pope Benedict XVI said that the true tree of life is the cross on which Jesus was crucified.

> "…the Cross is the true tree of life. We are not alive to become masters of life but to give it. Love is a giving of self, and this is why it is the way of true life, symbolized by the Cross."

The tree of life that Pope Benedict describes gives way to a life that is centered or rooted in love.

Imagine if we all lived our lives rooted in love and for the glory of God. I think if that were the case, we'd have a different swagger. Perhaps we'd stop being so hard on ourselves. Stop shaming ourselves. Stop being so mean and jealous towards others. Stop being so selfish and uncaring towards people who are different from us. Realizing you were created for glory and love sounds like the VIP experience, but it's not. It's a human experience available to all of us.

Date: 09/18/2017 | Placement: Left-back/shoulder. | Tattoo Artist: Mario
Delgado | Elements: Hebrew script "Die with memories, not dreams." Lion.

DIE WITH MEMORIES, NOT DREAMS

Paul

It was really late at night, and the television was flickering in the background. I couldn't sleep. My bravado had given way to fear. I was tired, so very tired. And scared, so very scared.

A few days shy of my forty-ninth birthday, with my health deteriorating fairly markedly, a friend had somehow finagled an appointment for me to meet with the world-renowned Dr. Thomas K. Szulc, MD, at his New York Center of Innovative Medicine. I'd traveled from Chicago to New York to see him with the fervent hope that he'd be willing and able to be additive to the mystics and mayhem approach I'd been taking towards not dying and regaining my health.

I felt that God's fingerprints were all over my initial visit. At first blush, I really liked and respected Dr. Tom. Based on the results from the cutting-edge Bioresonance Analysis of Health evaluation he performed, I trusted him when I was told what was wrong with me and how I might go about getting healthy again.

As dire as my situation sounded, I still smile when I look at the photograph I took of the notes I made the day I received my diagnosis. My brain, lungs, kidney, toxicity levels, viral and neural loads, parasites, amoeba, and flukes dominated line items #1 through #5... #6 was cancer progressing rapidly in my abdominal area #7 ditto for pancreas, bowel, and stomach #8 ditto for sinus and lymphatic system. Starting to feel a little overwhelmed at the detailed confirmation of what I'd been told piecemeal up 'till then, I drew some solace and stopped scribbling notes when assured, "We've seen a lot worse."

The folks at NYCIM wanted me to start treatment as soon as possible. But, first, I had a little bit of living left to do, namely getting a tattoo in San Francisco on my birthday from the remarkable Mario Delgado. Followed by a visit to the Amazon with my friend Yossi Ghinsberg to spend some time with revered healers and Pachemama.

The tattoo Mario inked was a lion surrounded by the phrase "Die with memories, not dreams." The lion idea was a blend of irony, homage, and motivation.

The irony was that I was the furthest thing from being the king of the jungle. I was a hot mess. I'd had a lot of moments when I was scared... really scared. I'd had a lot of moments, too, when I just felt so incredibly stupid. Having built a career and literally been published propagating the notion that stress is optional, here I was buckling and breaking under the allostatic load that I'd placed upon myself. I knew better, yet thinking that this kind of thing happened to other people, never happened to me, had led me to drop my guard. I was not doing the things I knew I should be doing if I didn't want to die unnecessarily or prematurely.

Homage and motivation to the lion were with respect to some of my military background and experience. Whilst a fairly nondescript soldier myself, over the years, I'd served, worked, and been associated with numerous men and women in the armed services whose fortitude and commitment to this day humbles and inspires me. So when moments arose when all I wanted to do was roll up in a ball in the corner and give up, my heritage and memories reminded and inspired me not to be a wuss.

And then there was the practical side of things. Forty-something years earlier, I'd been attacked by a lion cub. It was the first wild animal that'd attacked me. I'd lived. Over the years, crocodiles, hippopotamuses, and humans had joined the list of creatures that had tried to shorten my lifespan. They'd all failed, and I'd lived. There was no way in hell that I was going to let a bunch of amoebae, flukes, parasites, and pathogens take me down without a fight.

If I was going to die prematurely, I was going to arrive late to my deathbed, battered, and worn with memories of having done everything I could do to live, rather than resignedly crawling into said deathbed with dreams of what I coulda, shoulda, woulda done and the life I might have lived.

Rebecca

I don't care what I die with; I'll be dead.

The saying on Paul's lion tattoo felt cliché and meaningless to me. If anything, it felt like excuses for poor judgment, bad behavior, taking careless risks, and not saving for retirement. Then, for a moment, it got worse. He told me he was actually going to get two quotes tattooed with the Lion. The other (that didn't make it onto his back) was, "Not all who wander are lost." I wasn't sure. Should I be relieved or annoyed that the quote didn't make the cut? To me, those words seemed to give the green light to living a haphazard life and prompted sarcastic thoughts in me like; *I'm not really lost; I'm just wandering enjoying the day communing with creation and have no need to be responsible to or for anyone. Either way, I smugly thought, okay, great. I'll be over here with my GPS enjoying a swift route to my destination and dreams.*

Once I actually gave this tattoo (and potential tattoo) some thought, my mind went to the desert. As a churchy girl, I cannot help but associate the word "wander" with the 40 years the Israelites spent walking in the desert. For 40 years, they wandered about, hoping to eventually reach the Promised Land. As the Promised Land finally came into view, Moses, their leader, gave them a speech encouraging them to remember that their decades of wandering had led them to the Promised Land. Their initial motivation was to escape a life of slavery. Their dream was reaching the Promised Land. They had done both. Probably not under the conditions or circumstances they would have chosen, but they were on the brink of doing it!

Moses knew that, at times, these 40 years in the desert were so bad that people had wanted to return to slavery. The situation in the desert was so trying that rather than having their freedom in the desert, they began to think they'd be better off enslaved. They did not want to be in the desert anymore. They could not take it! The Israelites were so depleted and frustrated that they wanted to kill Moses for taking them on this excruciating journey. The very man that had once been their hero leading them out of slavery was now a villain.

Knowing their desire to return to slavery and plotting to kill Moses, it would be safe to say that they had had horrible desert experiences. However, they had a richer understanding and closer relationship with God because of their time in the desert. Moses seemed to understand these two things, but he wasn't sure if they realized how their 40 years of wandering had benefited their relationship with God.

As their wandering neared the end, everyone knew that while they had been freed from the Egyptians, this had not been a great time for anyone. Moses didn't want their desert experience, and likely all of his efforts, to go to waste. So, like any good leader does before a big game, meeting, or event, he gave them a pep talk. Just as they were about to enter the land of Canaan, Moses gathered them and delivered a speech to the Israelites.

As he preached to them, he encouraged the Israelites to remember. In Deuteronomy 8:1-20, Moses talks to the people gathered on the precipice of the Promised Land. This speech or sermon includes four imperative statements. Imperatives are used when we want to give instructions or orders to someone. Therefore, the use of four commands for them to remember to not forget in Moses' talk is significant.

At some point in their life, a parent undoubtedly says, "Make your bed." It's not a question or a statement that includes openness to the other's perspective or feelings about making the bed. The instruction is: make your bed. There is no sit-down or calendar invite sent "Making Bed Discussion" at 3:00 pm. Nope, there's no conversation. Just an imploring command from your parents to make your bed, or in this case, Moses encouraging everyone to remember the Lord. Remember the Lord. I mean, how hard is that? Moses, I do remember the Lord. Mom, making the bed isn't that big of a deal. So what if the sheets are strewn everywhere, and pillows are nestled amidst a haphazardly thrown duvet. Relax, Mom. Relax, Moses.

The repetitive commands of Moses to the people to remember are explicit. He wants them both to remember the Lord and, "Remember the long way that the LORD your God has led you" (Deuteronomy 8:2). It was as if, just in case some of them had blocked parts of this experience out, he wanted to cull out the memories from their consciousness.

In the book of Deuteronomy, Moses describes the terrain that he and the Israelites had traversed. He cements into their minds the experience they had all endured. In his words, their long way was a "great and terrible wilderness, an arid wasteland with poisonous snakes and scorpions" (Deuteronomy 8:15). It's safe to say anything that involves with poisonous snakes and scorpions is not an easy journey. This wasn't a stroll through the manicured grounds of Versailles. No, the Israelites had experienced a black diamond-level desert walk that went on and on and on. Moses did not want them to forget that God had led them out of this long, arduous situation. They didn't do this on their own; God was there. They were not to block out the snakes and scorpions. They were not to forget their hunger. They were not to forget the burning in their legs from walking up sand dunes. They were not to forget that some of them had been near death. Their "long way" was to be remembered.

Long ways or desert journeys are painfully unpleasant. The memories of long ways are also unpleasant. There are all kinds of possible reasons we set off on our long desert journeys. Maybe, like the Israelites, we were seeking freedom. Perhaps we were over-committed to a job or a toxic relationship. Maybe an addiction had taken hold of us.

The idea of getting to our own promised land is exciting. It's invigorating to think about getting free from a toxic job or relationship. Not relying on a drink or pain killer to get through the day is uplifting. At the beginning of our journeys, there is such optimism and unabashed hope for what our promised land will be like. It's incredibly exciting and energizing, but then days turn into weeks. The month on the calendar changes, pitchers and catchers report, the leaves change colors, a year or two pass. Hope has faded, and there is a realization that there isn't an expressway from Egypt to the Promised Land. There isn't an easy way to get over my divorce, addiction, or career change. I have to walk and work. Day in and day out, I have to look for a job, compose cover letters, send out countless resumes, and get rejected numerous times. Thoughts creep into our minds; *maybe my job isn't so bad after all?*

Taking the expressway through the Promised Land can take many forms. We look for shortcuts to sidestep the suffering, to quench our thirst in our desert wandering, we throwback shots of tequila, or perhaps some would more refinely sip on a nice glass of chardonnay. Or we gamble, over shop, overindulge in food, soothe ourselves with drugs, and in all kinds of other ways.

The Israelites did not have the option to sit at home and watch Netflix instead of attending a networking event. Instead, they had to keep walking. They didn't really know the way, nor did they know how long it would take them. They were the dry desert version of Dory: just keep walking, keep walking, and keep walking.

It took them 40 years. Some people didn't live through the journey. Others forged friendships relationships. No doubt, children were born. Things were celebrated and mourned. For some, journeying through the desert was the only life they had known. All of their memories would have included a desert landscape.

The Old Testament tells us that there were times when the Israelites wanted to go back. They almost killed Moses at some point because they had had enough of the hardship. It wasn't that he had done anything wrong. It was just hard, so very hard. All of this seemingly aimless wandering seemed worse than their known enslavement to the Egyptians.

I have had my own long way. Thankfully it did not span 40 years. Despite my truncated desert journey, there were times when I took shortcuts. These didn't work. They weren't effective and just masked the suffering I was feeling. They didn't move me forward at all. They just created a desert mirage. A false sense that I had succeeded. I had not. That everything was okay. Everything was not.

God felt far away from me in my desert moments. The poisonous snakes in my life seemed closer and more interested in me than God did. Yet, I can see that as was the case with the Israelites, God was present with me the entire time.

We might not have a leader like Moses to give us a speech as our arduous journeys level out, but we can hold onto Moses' words to the Israelites. Moses preemptively cautions the Israelites against pride and self-sufficiency in his speech filled with imperatives. He tells them not to get too full of themselves as they settle into the Promised Land. After they arrive, they are not to forget about the manna God had provided or the steadfastness and guidance of God during their 40 years in the desert. In short, he tells them: Hey, remember you were dependent on God, and it worked out. Now that you've made it through the desert, don't get too full of yourselves and think you don't need God anymore.

We navigate challenging terrain and go through desert moments in our life. God is there for us, too, guiding us in our wandering, supporting us in our difficult times. As they wandered for forty years, the Israelites had nothing but God. As it turns out, that may be all you need to reach the promised land.

Date: 10/21/2017 | Placement: Right ribs. | Art: Gabriel Wolffe from Hebrew Tattoos | Tattoo Artist: Aura Dalian 03/22/2019 | Elements: Hebrew script in the shape of a cross. "Only God should judge." "Kindness begets kindness." Flowers.

ONLY GOD SHOULD JUDGE. KINDNESS BEGETS KINDNESS

Paul

If God judges me and keeps score of my transgressions, and that determines whether I end up in heaven or hell, I'm screwed. With all the mistakes I've made, sins I've committed, and all the things I've messed up either intentionally or unintentionally, all the things I've done, and all the things I've failed to do... ooh la la, it's going to be real toasty in the afterlife.

In much the same way, when I judge and keep scores of my own and other people's transgressions, we're all screwed. Very little good comes from that. It doesn't feel good and isn't a pretty look on anybody. We all make mistakes, some of which we regret and wish we could undo. Some we learn from. Some we don't. Regardless, for something to be judged or seen as a mistake, it has to have happened in the past, and thus we have no real control over it. We do have influence over what happens next; that's entirely up to us and being judgmental and experiencing or inflicting suffering is optional, as is being kind.

Getting back to God. Fortunately for me, my God is kind, tolerant, forgiving, and has a sense of humor. I believe that He/She/It has my back and is a huge fan of Karma (cause and effect). It seems that, for the most part, when I do things that are going to hurt me or someone else, they hurt. On the other hand, when I'm kind to myself and others, more often than not, it feels good to me and seemingly feels good and inspires them to be kind too. Unfortunately, sometimes I forget this simple truism, and it invariably bites me on the butt when I do.

At the time I got this tattoo, I was in the midst of living a pretty full life that included being a parent, running a few businesses and a foundation, as well as navigating and hopefully side-stepping a potential death sentence whilst reluctantly accepting my impending divorce. In my quest for life over death, I was in the midst of a fairly intense treatment protocol at the New York Center of Innovative Medicine and had flown into Detroit for the weekend to be with my kids.

The tattoo I'd asked Gabriel at Hebrew Designs to design was a cross that said, "Only God should judge" and "Kindness begets kindness." My relationship with God was complicated at the time. However, my relationship with the concept of *kindness bringing kindness* is unshakable. The renowned Aura Dalian had agreed to work with me again, incorporating watercolors and meaningful wildflowers into the design. The flowers and the watercolors represent things that are important to me, my children, the land of my birth, people in my life, and Pachamama, AKA Earth Mother.

When I say my relationship with God was complicated, it was. As the product of a good Catholic education gone awry due to a curious mind, many and varied experiences as I've bumbled along through life, and a particularly wonderful dalliance with Buddhism, my predominantly Christian faith is firmly entrenched as the keystone of my existence. My relationship with God, akin to that of a very best friend, under duress, can be complicated. I believe wholeheartedly in the God of my understanding and am a fan of the Bible. I've also learned a lot from the people and texts of other religions and belief structures that I've encountered along the way. I have the utmost respect for everyone else's beliefs and, for the most part, feel pretty comfortable with my own.

As a big-time, longtime fan of God, I'm occasionally surprised by some people's need to tell me that I'm wrong about Him/Her/It. I may well be. It's not uncommon for me to be told that I've misunderstood what I've been taught about a lot of things, most relevant to this part of our conversation, the narratives surrounding the cross and the crucifixion.

When I see the cross, I can't help but smile when I consider how the God of my understanding nailed it when it comes to revealing the oxymoronic relationship that exists between free will and Divine intervention.

In my story, my God orchestrated events such that his son, JC, chose to suffer unimaginably so that I don't have to. As a result, during challenging times, I can leave my baggage, fears, insecurities, and resentments at the foot of the cross whenever I choose to and, provided I'm authentically contrite, if I've done something wrong or been a jerk, all will be forgiven. Then, with insights gained and lessons learned, I can freely and wholeheartedly get back into the fray that is so often my life and explore the untold possibilities availed to me. Or I can choose to hang onto all the BS – dragging my baggage, my fears, insecurities, and resentments along with me as I trudge through life, rendering my day-to-day experience so much more difficult than it needs to be, and the chances of doing God's will: slim to zip.

Unfortunately, I have my human moments, and sometimes it all just gets a little overwhelming. Occasionally I'd catch myself dragging my baggage and wallowing in brief but intense bouts of heroic suffering. Then, I'd get all pissed off, singing the woe is me ballad and judging the bejesus out of people.

When wallowing, I'd throw up a list of grievances that I was all too happy to share with anyone who'd listen. Deep down, I knew that no one really wanted to listen to me bitch, moan, snivel, and whine about my lot in life. I knew that I was being an energy vamp and abusing their care, goodwill, and patience. It was just too easy for me to point my finger elsewhere, for me to judge and blame everyone and everything else, including God and the universe, for whatever wasn't working out in my life the way I wanted it to. At times it was way easier to be a whiny little bitch who was seemingly more committed to being a victim and being right than I was to being me and to being responsible, kind, and happy. In these moments, my long-suffering family and friends would often sift through the drama, remind me of the facts whilst granting me a sympathetic ear. They could see that I was navigating a pretty messed-up situation, and they cared and wanted to help.

There's a cautionary adage, "To fall asleep more easily, don't let a good story get in the way of the facts." Looking back, I wish I'd paid better attention to the counsel the adage offered. In trying to make sense of situations in my life that made no sense to me — particularly my health and my family disintegrating. I let myself get overwhelmed and afraid. I let too many stories get in the way of what was actually going on — the facts.

Particularly insidious narratives were the ones centered on times I coulda, shoulda, woulda been a better husband, lived a more wholesome life, not been so ambitious and driven. Given half a chance, whilst fighting to fall asleep, I could come up with really compelling stories of how I was wrong, bad, at fault, and the primary cause of all of my suffering. But, objectivity being elusive, I lost sleep, and my physical, mental, and emotional health suffered.

Whenever casting myself as either the victim or the villain in my stories, I'd usually let myself get carried away and caught up in all the drama. As a result, I'd lose sight of the facts that either by what I'd done or by what I'd failed to do, I had contributed, often unwittingly, towards much — but not all — of the suffering that I was experiencing in any given situation.

Sometimes I was able to catch myself being myself take a few breaths, step back from the drama and be honest with myself. It was awesome to let myself see things as they actually were versus how I was seeing them or how I wanted them to be. I could usually see both where I'd messed things up and what I could do to fix them. I could see opportunities to be responsible and productively choose to accept that I am the primary cause of the results of my actions and inactions, my experience of life, and to a large degree, others' experiences and opinions of me.

In those moments, I'd get curious as cognitively I knew that only God should judge and that kindness brings kindness. When I embodied these notions, suffering was optional. I was pretty good at talking the talk, but I sometimes struggled with walking the walk.

I love looking at my tattoo and being reminded that only God should judge, and kindness begets kindness. I accept, without reservation, that my life is way better when I stop trying to control everything and instead leave all the judging of myself, other people, places, and things to God and my baggage, fears, insecurities, and resentments at the foot of the cross. There's a wonderful juxtaposition of free will blending with Divine intervention when I'm kind to myself and others. When that happens, things seem to work out better for them and for me than when I don't.

Rebecca

I am aware of two or three absolutes in life. One of which is that I am going to die. While I don't know that I need a tattoo to remind me of that, the images of the cross and flowers made up of the words, "Only God should judge" and "Kindness begets kindness," seem like a great reminder of how to live one's life before it's over.

I am not one of those people who tells others not to waste their money buying me flowers. However, I will echo the words of a Tanya Tucker lyric, "Bring my flowers now while I'm living." Don't waste your money on flowers once I'm gone, but for the time being, while I'm a breathing being, please shower me with those fresh-cut stems. Giving flowers to myself or others is just the beginning of kindness begets kindness. Whether they are from someone else or a gift from myself, having a blooming bouquet within my sight really does make me smile. Whether it's buying yourself an occasional grocery store bouquet, letting yourself binge watch Netflix, or giving yourself a pep talk, it's important to remember that we are to be kind to ourselves as well as others.

I've discovered that I'm kinder to others when I am kind to myself. There's no sense in being hard on myself or judging myself if it doesn't make me good at being myself. This doesn't mean that I let myself off the hook or that I am allowed to act however I want because "I'm just being me." What it does mean is that in each action, word, and choice I have the option of being kind or not. No matter how much sleep we have not gotten, how hungry we are, or what our workload is, we always have the choice to act with kindness.

In my mind, kindness does not equal being nice. Unfortunately, sometimes when we act with kindness, people don't get what they want or get upset with us. I am kind to myself by occasionally writing inspirational notes in dry erase marker on my bathroom mirror, taking myself to the gym, or making myself go home and not staying out to do more shots. There are days when I don't want to go to the gym. Making myself workout does not feel nice. However, in order to have a shot at a healthy life in which I avoid clogged arteries and type 2 diabetes, I work out. That is being kind to my future self.

Teaching my frustrated nephew, Asher, that he shouldn't cheat doesn't feel nice for him at that moment because he really, really wants to be the winner. Even though it's just Uno, I would be an unkind aunt if I perpetuated his cheating behavior in the name of being nice. In these circumstances, it can be hard to follow through on kindness. My friends may get mad at me if I go home early, or my nephew won't want to play with me if he cannot get away with cheating. Of course, I want to make my friends happy and my nephew to like me. However, more importantly, I want my friends and me to be safe and wake up with at least a chance of not being incredibly sleep-deprived and hungover the day after our night out. Even more so, I want Asher to grow into an honest man with integrity.

The two phrases intertwined on the cross depicted in Paul's tattoo, "Only God should judge" and "Kindness begets kindness," remind us that leaving kindness behind and leading with judgment is unproductive.

These seven words in Paul's tattoo form a cross. In Catholicism, the sign of the cross is how we begin prayers. In the sacrament of baptism, a cross in holy oil is traced over those being initiated into Christianity. The cross gives us the greatest event in Christianity. Christianity teaches that the salvation of humanity is a result of Jesus' resurrection after his death on a cross. The rising that came three days after his horrible and agonizing death on the cross is a gift. One that I don't deserve. One that I didn't earn. It's better than those fresh-cut flowers. The love that God gives to humanity through the cross is unimaginable.

Jesus left judgment out of the cross equation. Even while nailed to the cross, he didn't judge others and wasn't mean to those in his presence. From where I'm sitting, I would think that Jesus had every right to be upset with the Roman authorities who sentenced him to death or with the soldiers who mocked and beat him on the way to his execution. Yet, we don't hear any reports of Jesus lashing out or acting judgmental to these people.

Jesus even acted with kindness and remained in a judgment-free zone with those nailed to their crosses on each side of him. If there were ever a moment to act unkind or to be judgmental, this would have been it. Jesus had been crucified and was no doubt in unfathomable pain from the nails tearing through his flesh, organs, and bones. Yet, when a man beside him asked for help, for Jesus to save him, Jesus did not say, "Shut up, shut up!

Take care of yourself! You got yourself in this situation, didn't you?" No, he does not do that. Luke's gospel tells us that instead, Jesus told the man that he would be with him in paradise.

After the humiliating agony of his crucifixion on the cross, Christianity says that Jesus rose from the dead. After his time on the cross and resurrection, Jesus makes himself present to people who had abandoned him while he was there. Again, he is not upset with his friends and followers who questioned his resurrection. He accepts doubting Thomas when Thomas doesn't believe that it is Jesus standing in front of him. Jesus is concerned about them getting the message. He wants them to have understanding and faith. He's not concerned about being right or being better than them (even though, as God, he is!). He's not worried about how they are different than he is. He doesn't care about their political party affiliation. He's not concerned about their outfits or their occupations. He's concerned that they know he rose from the dead and that God's love for humanity is infinite.

We don't know the crosses that people carry with them. Be kind to others. We simply don't know. Is the bitter and angry person in line with me at the grocery store sad and hurt because they just found out their spouse is having an affair? Is the agitated person in the elevator sleep deprived because they were up all night caring for their sick child or aging parent? The person who seems cold and standoffish may be suffering from anxiety.

We can be hard on ourselves and hard on others. We all sin and yet often feel more comfortable judging others for what we see as bad or wrong in them than looking for areas of improvement in ourselves. Judging others is almost like thinking our sins or shortcomings are less egregious than those we see in someone else. We are all flawed (that's why we needed Jesus on the cross in the first place).

It's also important not to judge ourselves too harshly. We are works in progress. God constantly calls us and cultivates us into who we are meant to be. This takes some learning. Life and lessons need to be experienced, not just posted in pithy sayings on social media. We aren't perfect, but God loves us and gave us something even better than flowers that afternoon on the cross. That's another one of those absolutes that I'm aware of.

Date: 11/29/2017 & 05/28/2018 | Placement: Left chest. | Tattoo
Artist: Amanda 11/29/2017 | Tattoo Artist: Aura Dalian 05/28/2018
| Elements: Lotus flowers. Butterflies. Ribbon. Semi-colon.

LOTUS FLOWERS. BUTTERFLIES. RIBBON. SEMI-COLON

Paul

B ack in Kathmandu, we were shooting stock footage in a downtown bazaar. There was a lot of poverty all around us. Nepal is breathtakingly beautiful in places, but there is a lot of abject poverty on the flip side of that beauty. It seemed that there was a lot of suffering going on all over the place, and I was growing calloused to it. I'm a little embarrassed to admit that I was learning how to walk past the beggars and the waifs, looking past or straight through them as they begged, threatened, or pleaded for help.

Which is what made what happened next kinda curious. We were passing through a narrow alley, having broken free of a throng of beggars, when a lady worked her way up to me. She was of indeterminate age and wearing the uniform of the poor, the lowly, the downtrodden, the destitute. There was no doubt in my mind whatsoever that life had been extremely hard and most likely exceptionally cruel to this woman. ... and yet there was something about her. Something about her energy, her posture, the way she held her head up and looked me square in the eyes and in broken English, asked humbly yet passionately, "Sir, please will you help my children?" There was something about her that captured my attention. "Sure." We entered the supply store she was standing in front of. "Who are you, and what do you need?" In somewhat broken English I learned a little more about this mysteriously enthralling woman.

Her name was Vimla. She, her sister, and ten children were struggling to get by. We got baby formula and enough essential supplies to feed a gaggle of cheerleaders. Putting the food in bags, I wished her Godspeed, but she was having none of that. Instead, she insisted that she take me, Kim, and the film crew to her home to meet her family and share a cup of tea with us. There was no getting out of it, particularly once Kim agreed.

The journey to Vimla's home was quite a trek, we left the bazaar and trudged towards the city garbage dump.

In the garbage dump was a house made out of garbage. Ducking my head and squinting my eyes as Kim and I entered Vimla's home, we came face to face with her family. Her sister and all their kids. It turns out that they had lived in neighboring India. Let's just say, as products of arranged marriages, Vimla, and her sister had barely survived a difficult past. It'd gotten to the point where escaping by foot and walking from their village in India, across the mountains, all the way to Kathmandu had seemed their only viable option if the two women and their children were going to even have a shot at a life they felt was worth living.

They completed the arduous journey, and because Vimla could speak some English, they'd made the executive decision that her sister was going to build and then stay home and take care of the kids whilst Vimla was going to work and earn some money. Vimla is an intelligent, driven, beautiful woman. At first, things looked like they were going to work out. The women had enough money between them to buy supplies to start a shoeshine business, and things were going according to plan. Until the day Vimla was brutally beaten, assaulted, and robbed of everything she possessed. Once she was well enough to work, she tried really hard to find any job. Securing employment, particularly without the requisite paperwork, turned out to be more of a challenge than even Vimla was prepared for. She was reduced to doing whatever she needed to do in order to make enough money to keep her family alive.

I can only imagine the strength of character and fortitude it must have taken for her to live the life she lived. The life of abuse, the life of beatings, the life of objectification, of being used and discarded. Vimla did what she needed to do to survive. Sometimes she did it in increments of one breath at a time. She did what she needed to do to keep her family alive. As hours rolled into days, weeks, months, and years her love of and commitment to her family was all that kept her alive.

I sat listening to this tale, told not by a victim but by someone proud of who she was and what she had done. A mother, a sister, an aunt who loved and took care of her family, doing whatever she could, whatever she needed to do to support their survival. I was just blown away, as was Kim.

Kim wears her emotions on her sleeve, and I could tell that Vimla and her family had really gotten to her. At that moment, we decided to award the micro-grant to Vimla and her family. We couldn't help a lot, but we could help enough.

The overarching intent of my foundation's micro-grant program was to find people who, given that we were in Nepal and using the lotus flower as a metaphor may have been rooted in the dirt but were going to blossom. Once we found them, we were committed to helping them live with dignity and supporting their entrepreneurial success. The model we used was incredibly simple – provide micro-grants and some strategic and pragmatic support to set up income-generating projects that would enhance the livelihoods of the people directly involved and those in their care. Our hope was that the people running these social enterprises would then pay it forward.

To me, Vimla was like a beautiful lotus flower. She may have started rooted deep in mud and scum, but I saw in her the potential to blossom and make her way through the murky water until she finally broke the surface, emerging and blooming in the sun, beautiful and whole.

Vimla ran with the opportunity afforded to her. She worked her way into a home, a room with an address that enabled her to get her kids into school and an education. After a few false starts – one of which included her being badly beaten and all her work product stolen again – with Kim and my foundation's help, she set up a business making beautiful handcrafts which were sold both in Kathmandu and in the United States.

Vimla found other women who had similar backstories. Collectively, they were magnificent. They went on to establish a successful social enterprise. The women created jobs with livable incomes. Their kids were getting fed and educated, and life was seemingly trending in the right direction. Their journey had many ups and downs with some pretty precarious learning curves. Some hurt. Some healed. Some just were. Kim and Vimla got the Nepal Women's Empowerment Social Enterprise Project up and running.

They were self-sufficient, no longer needed funding, and with everything else going on in my life, they fell off my radar.

Fast forward a few years to May 9th, 2020. It was the day before Mother's Day, and we were in the grips of the global pandemic. Kim called. She'd just seen Vimla on the television news. With COVID-19 ravaging her village, she had started an initiative to help feed people. She'd raised enough money to fill an entire truck with food which she portioned out and was able to feed just over 300 families.

Vimla, the caterpillar who'd crossed our path, had morphed into a beautiful butterfly. Kim calls her God's silent server. I think of her as an exemplar of the inspirational nature of the human spirit, a reminder that if we care about each other and are willing to give each other a chance and a helping hand, then anything is possible.

I'll be eternally grateful to Vimla for showing me how humility and vulnerability are superpowers. From time to time, we all need help, and when we do, it's okay to ask for it. I'm thankful to her, too, for the reminders that it doesn't matter how bad or hopeless things seem or what restrictions we appear to be shackled by or limitations have been placed upon us, we always have the freedom of choice. It doesn't matter how often or how hard we get knocked down. All that matters, in the end, is whether or not we choose to get back up. If we get up one more time than we fall, we will make it through.

When I look at my tattoo, the lotus flowers remind me that we all go through hell, through the mud and the mire, that at various times in our lives we all suffer, and it sucks. But, more often than not, if we keep going, if we're grateful, kind, and just keep doing the next right thing, then we will break the surface and blossom, beautiful and whole. The red lotus on my tattoo reminds me to love and be compassionate, and the blue one to think things through before doing them.

The butterflies on my tattoo remind me that I can leave my old life behind and begin a new one whenever I want to. They remind me that change and transformation are inevitable and that confidence, courage, hope, renewal, resilience, forgiveness, and freedom are optional and eminently accessible if I choose them to be.

The lavender semicolon cancer ribbon reminds me when I need it that my story isn't over yet.

Rebecca

The lavender semi-colon cancer ribbon looks a bit out of place in this tattoo. The colorful depiction of butterflies and lotus flowers dominates this image. The connection becomes apparent to me as I realize that there have been many moments in life when I thought things were finished. Over. Period, the end. However, these have actually turned into semi-colon moments of blooming metamorphosis.

In writing, semicolons link two clauses or two different ideas together. The followers of Jesus likely thought his crucifixion was a period and not a semicolon. Their leader had been the recipient of the death penalty. Upon hearing that Jesus was killed, his disciples and close followers ran off and hid. They were frightened. Understandably so, they didn't want to be next. They likely couldn't conceive that this would not be the end of things for them and Jesus. I would guess that following the crucifixion of Jesus they huddled hidden in the upper room, sad, scared, grieving, and wondering where they were to go from here. Yet, three days later, Jesus rose from the dead and made an appearance to them, providing them with the ultimate semicolon moment.

Prior to his crucifixion, Jesus had not left them a manual. He did, however, leave them with stories and lessons. Jesus gave them the experiences of interacting with unclean people, gathering with those on the margins of society, and having conversations with the outcasts. Before his crucifixion, his close companions shared in moments of healing and prayer with Jesus. It was up to them to translate those experiences and lessons from Jesus into their life and faith following his crucifixion and resurrection.

Crucifixion is a dramatic event. I am not a dramatic person. However, my brain does send out some sort of signal that the emotions I am experiencing are probably going to cause my death. Even when I think my death is likely pending due to the hurt and agony, I see in the world or the departure of a husband, I keep it together. I quietly retreat like an animal in the woods. I don't make a big fuss. I get my affairs in order. Make sure my beneficiaries are up to date. I straighten my place up a little, but not too much because if I die, I don't care about leaving a small mess behind.

As it turns out, I have not died from any of my emotions. The periods that I thought life was giving me turned out to be semicolons. One of the most extreme feelings of impending death that I felt was in early 2019. My second husband told me that he wanted a divorce and was moving out. This news came less than eighty days after we closed on a condo we had purchased together. Suffice it to say; this news was a surprise. It wasn't a surprise because we had an amazing marriage. It was a surprise because I thought he would never leave. Our marriage was a mix of good as well as some very painful and unhealthy patterns and experiences. I think it was to the relief of my friends and family that this marriage came to an end. While they knew I was heartbroken and devastated over the loss of the relationship, they knew it was better for me. They, unlike me, had confidence that my life would improve. This was not a period but a semicolon in the story of my life.

I surrounded myself with quotes, "Everything is going to be alright, maybe not today, but eventually." "Every setback is a setup for a comeback." They left little impact on my flattened and destroyed heart. Then a rush of pain would envelop me. I'd wonder, "*What is that? I'm here alone. Sitting still. How can I hurt this badly?*"

As months passed and 2020 appeared on the calendar page, I felt like a massive success story. *I had not died.* In fact, in my mind, I had achieved something spectacular!! I felt as though I had just climbed Mount Everest without oxygen. My spectacular feat was that I had survived divorce! I had lived through the heart-wrenching, overwhelmingly painful process of divorce. Realizing I had lived shifted something in me. I started to think about my life, the world, what I wanted to do, and how I wanted to spend my time.

The transformation of a caterpillar into a butterfly, the emergence of a clean lotus flower out of the muddy soil, a semicolon; the images in this tattoo as illustrations of transformation are abundant. We as humans may be similar to a caterpillar in that we might not see our metamorphosis coming! I know for me, one day, I was crawling along (on fewer legs than a caterpillar) painfully making my way through the post-divorce terrain of my life without any notion of metamorphosis as I was just trying to live. And yet, less than a year later, I was flying through life in much less pain as a very different creature.

As a child, I caught numerous caterpillars and "cared" for them in a large mason jar while I awaited their metamorphosis. As a hostess in training, I created a nice environment for their metamorphosis. The lid of the jar had several holes in it. There were green sprigs of trees and bushes in the jar. And as directed by my parents, a stick for the butterfly to eventually hang its cocoon.

Likely to the disappointment of my science teacher, I still don't quite understand how one day this black and yellow crawling creature formed a cocoon and then became a black and orange winged butterfly. They are two completely different creatures! The colors are different. Their textures are different. Butterflies are delicate and beautiful in a way caterpillars are not. Butterflies can fly! Caterpillars crawl and make their way over the ground with multiple legs. Does a butterfly find flying exciting, or do they miss all of those legs they had as a caterpillar? It seems as though caterpillars don't have a choice in their metamorphosis. They are destined only to be a caterpillar for so long, and then they will, ready or not, turn into a butterfly. Scientists believe that caterpillars aren't aware that as their life progresses, they are going to metamorphose into a butterfly. A caterpillar must experience a metamorphosis. If it doesn't create a cocoon and go through its metamorphosis, it will inevitably die. To keep living, it must change.

Just because we go through a transformation doesn't mean we forget what our life was like before. For example, the followers of Jesus took their experiences with him and carried those lessons out to the world after his resurrection. Likewise, scientists have studied the brains of butterflies to determine that they too take their experiences as caterpillars into their lives as butterflies.

A metamorphosis gives us a new way of seeing things. New boundaries. A new sense of gratitude. We have changed. Maybe we have gotten a new haircut, taken up a new hobby or let go of that unhealthy relationship. Perhaps we are now drinking champagne because our pre-metamorphosis lifestyle is no longer our cup of tea. No matter the outcome of our metamorphosis, as we take flight, we take with us the lessons we learned while crawling.

Date: 12/02/2017 | Placement: Right outer bicep. | Tattoo
Artist: Mario Delgado | Elements: Mary Magdalene.

MARY MAGDALENE

Paul

Note: Some of the names have been changed to protect the identity of some of the people who were kind enough to help me.

My dear friend Yossi Ginsberg and I met up in La Paz, Bolivia. Extraordinarily a few years earlier, Yossi had gotten lost in the Amazon jungle and had survived for more than three weeks on his own with nothing more than his mind, heart, and the clothes he wore. A bona fide survivor, he was bound and determined that I should live. Yossi introduced me to both the jungle and the healers who'd played such instrumental parts in shaping his survival and his life.

The first person Yossi wanted me to meet was Donna Emma, a respected and beloved healer who'd been crucial to his survival and return to health and wellbeing. Donna Emma and her granddaughter Maria, an oncologist from Cuba, welcomed me into their lives and to their family as we embarked upon a healing experience extraordinaire.

Having navigated my eclectic healing journey and frantically searched the globe for anything that could possibly help my daughter, Erin, I was extremely open to and familiar with what some might term "alternative modalities." The ancient healing arts and the power and versatility of Mother Nature (Pachamama) not only seemed plausible, their promise, probable. I really don't know how to convey the depth and breadth of my experiences in the Amazon. I probably don't ever want to know what I ate, drank, and had rubbed into my body. The things I saw, the things I did, ranged from the sublime to the ridiculous and the Divine to the miraculous. It was… well… it was freakin' awesome as the proven healing effects of the Amazon and Pachamama's mind-blowing cornucopia of herbs and potions coupled with the love and support of the people I met did what they were able to do.

Donna Emma would encourage me to spend some time at the La Paz Cathedral, also known as The Cathedral Basilica of Our Lady of Peace, between healings. Then, each day I'd return for my treatments and share with her my experiences and conversations with Mary Magdalene.

For the sake of accuracy, I should probably use the word communion instead of conversation, as it's the word that most clearly describes what happened. To me, the word communion means the sharing or exchanging of intimate thoughts and feelings, especially when the exchange is on a mental or spiritual level. However, I use the word conversation in my description because that's how I remember it.

The first time I sat and prayed in the cathedral, I became aware of someone next to me. She wore a nondescript headscarf and robe and had voluptuous blood-red lips. I was sitting there praying to God. Actually, there was a fair bit of bartering going on as I acknowledged what a shit I'd been in this life and begged (a) for forgiveness and (b) for healing. In return, I committed to mending my ways – with the caveat that God was open to stepping in and giving me a helping hand as needed. Given my history and experience, I knew I'd be needing a lot of help.

You see, I'm not a saint, nor have I ever claimed to be one. In this life, I've made more than my fair share of dodgy and questionable decisions. I've been known to drink, shag, smoke, dabble with drugs, eat badly, over-commit, under-deliver, over-party, and on occasion, be a real jerk. I've loved some too much and some not enough. Some of my actions and inactions have led to people dying before they otherwise might have and enabled others to keep living when maybe it'd have been better for the greater good if they'd died. I've made so many mistakes that have led to me hurting people and along the way have hurt myself a lot too. Sitting in God's House, considering all of this and reflecting on the seven deadly sins: lust, gluttony, greed, sloth, wrath, envy, and pride. Seven for seven, baby.

With all these thoughts tormentedly swirling around my mind and feeling lower than shark shit, I turned to the lass next to me. Not knowing what question to ask or what to say, I said nothing.

She smiled and, in her indeterminate accent, whispered conspiratorially, "It's going to be okay." For some unfathomable reason, I believed her. Thus began my conversations, my communion, with Mary Magdalene.

Our commune began with me verbally vomiting an unflattering hotch-potch of heroic suffering and righteous indignation. I was finding it way easier to blame everyone and everything else for the bad things that had happened or were going on in my life than to take responsibility for them myself. Given everything that was going on, I was at the same time angry, exhausted, indignant, lonely, offended, and desperate. My stress level redlining, harmful biomarkers presumably off the chart, and immune system becoming more and more and more compromised as the seconds ticked by, things were not going well for me. I sure as hell wasn't helping myself by thinking the thoughts I was thinking, being the ways that I was being, saying the things I was saying, or doing the things that I was doing.

Mary listened patiently for a while before kindly asking how all the crap I was sprouting was working for me? She asked how being so wrapped up in and held prisoner by all those stories was helping me to get from where I was to where I was trying to go. I was really sick and scared and claimed I wanted to live and take care of my children. Did it really matter what others had done or were doing to me? Did it really matter what others had said or were saying about me? Did it really matter what others thought about me or how they portrayed or treated me?

We discussed how history had not been kind to her either. How sometimes, innocently and inadvertently and sometimes with malicious intent, people had said things that had led to misunderstandings and misconceptions about her that had gone on to further birth falsehoods and, on occasion, intentional out-and-out bald-faced lies. As a result, a lot of people believed she was a hooker and/or that she'd shagged Jesus, and they didn't take too kindly to either belief. Unfortunately, this BS had not only colored what some people thought about her, but also had sadly removed the possibility of those very same people having any kind of relationship with the real Mary or deriving any comfort, insight, or value from her experiences that might otherwise have helped them or enriched their lives.

I could relate to Mary's experiences. Sitting there in a cathedral in La Paz, my attitude towards a lot of the people we talked about, from Pope Gregory the Great (the bloke largely responsible for misrepresenting Mary) to some of the people who were seemingly intent on making my life more challenging as I navigated my illness and my divorce, was *to hell with 'em.* Mary encouraged me not to go there but rather to acknowledge, accept, and have compassion for people who, driven by their agendas – sometimes from a place of fear, sometimes from a place of ignorance, and sometimes from a place of pride – will hide or alter the truth. They don't let the facts get in the way of the stories they're trying to sell to themselves and others. She invited me to look at people through a lens of love rather than a need to be right, to consider that sometimes people need to invent and live with lies because they can't live with the truth. If that's the case, then that's between them and God.

My to hell with 'em attitude manifesting as heroic suffering, righteous indignation, and blame with correlating red-lining stress and harmful bio-markers would be a great "How To Kill Yourself Quickly" case study in the medical field of psychoneuroimmunology, the study of the effect of the mind on health and resistance to disease. By allowing myself to get so uptight, I further compromised my already overstretched immune system. It was quite literally killing me. Mary jokingly pointed out that she thought I was smarter than that and invited me to remember that when people don't tell the truth about us, it reveals more about them than it does about us and that getting stressed about it all is optional.

To me, Mary inspiringly embodied unfathomable levels of acceptance and humility towards those who knocked her down for the sake of their agendas, who insisted on making her look bad for the sake of promoting their belief, cause, and/or identity. She also taught me that humility can be bad assed.

Whilst in Bolivia and upon my return to the United States, I collaborated with my new friend, Mario Delgado, one of San Francisco's most sought-after tattoo artists. His rendering of Mary Magdalene, the spitting image of what she looks like to me, still takes my breath away. It is a cherished reminder of our communion.

Rebecca

The removal of Paul's shirt revealed a rather sizable tattoo of an attractive woman. I don't know much about tattoos, but I know that women tattooed on men's arms are likely to be important women in the life of the arm's owner. Paul only has one arm. This made me think that the woman he chose to adorn this precious and limited tattoo real estate with must be very important.

When I initially saw the woman on Paul's arm, I was a bit taken aback by her beautiful countenance. Most men who make the decision to adorn their body with an important lady in their life choose either their mom or their significant other. This lady didn't look like someone's mom. Her beauty, particularly her lips, were a bit worrisome to me. Her lips were fierce! Uh-oh... my lips are my best physical feature. Are her lips better than my lips? My head was exploding with the question, *who is this lady? This woman with the great bone structure, flowing hair, and full lips, who is she, Paul?!* I inquired (hopefully) nonchalantly, "Tell me about this tattoo." It was then that I learned that it was Mary Magdalene.

Mary Magdalene!

In graduate school, Mary Magdalene had shown up for me in New Testament studies and Feminist Theology courses. However, Mary Magdalene had never been brought up in a conversation I'd had about tattoos!

Mary Magdalene is the second most mentioned woman in the Bible. Only Mary, the mother of Jesus, beats her out, winning the title for most mentioned female in the New Testament. I think if you're going to come in second place, finishing behind the mother of the Lord is a good spot to land. I also have to think that Mary Magdalene is not coming in with the first-place ribbon of all the women being tattooed on men's arms. Mary Magdalene is a New Testament rock star. She is consistently portrayed in the crucifixion and resurrection scenes in all four Gospels (it's not an easy feat to get Biblical consistency from all four evangelists). She is also unique in that she is the only woman in the Christian Scriptures who is named without relation to anyone else. She is not listed as someone's mother, wife, or daughter. Instead, her moniker includes only her hometown of Magdala. This likely indicates that she was a woman of prominence in this town situated on the banks of the Sea of Galilee.

For most of the centuries that followed Mary Magdalene's life, an unflattering rumor followed her around until the 20th century. Like the rumor on the TV show "Friends" didn't prevent Rachel Green from being a popular high school student, the rumor about Mary Magdalene hasn't prevented her from being important to Christianity. However, it likely makes her misunderstood and miscast.

At the end of the 6th century, Pope Gregory the Great misinformed people or started a rumor, so to speak, that Mary Magdalene was a prostitute. At that time, there was confusion over the identity of Mary Magdalene, Mary of Bethany, and an unnamed female sinner in Luke's gospel. (Confusion over identity doesn't seem to be an issue of gender as there has been similar confusion within the Church over the many Johns in the New Testament.) There was clarity about Mary, the mother of Jesus, but the Church blended Mary of Bethany and an unnamed sinful woman in Luke 7 into the person of Mary Magdalene.

Pope Gregory made the sexist leap that both the seven demons expelled from Mary Magdalene (Luke 8:1-3) and the unnamed woman's sin in Luke 7 were sexual sins. While making this grievous and ignorant error, Pope Gregory did seem to be acting out of a well-intended space. I'm not sure if he knows where the road paved with good intentions leads, but while preaching the homily that contained this error, he was trying to convey the message to the faithful that God forgave their sins. Good news for the crowd who heard his homily on a fall day in 591 CE, but bad news for the reputation of Mary Magdalene.

A long-overdue correction of her occupation occurred at the Second Vatican Council. In 1969 the Catholic Church admitted Pope Gregory's error and stated that she was, in fact, not a prostitute (yay?).

Most importantly, Mary Magdalene was the person who did not abandon Jesus. She was beside him in his life, at his death, and his resurrection. Her presence in these scenes of the life of Jesus cannot be disputed. What was she thinking as she heard Jesus' stories, as she ate with him, and saw the impact he had on others? As she sat at Calvary, knowing that her friend was about to be killed, what was she thinking? Perhaps she wasn't thinking but was feverishly praying for Jesus and those crucified alongside him. Maybe she was praying that the Roman authorities would change their minds and not crucify him, praying that he wouldn't die, praying that he wouldn't suffer. She was praying and praying into the evening, faced with the reality that the crucifixion and painful execution of Jesus had occurred. Perhaps the next day, she had thoughts of *God; you didn't listen to my prayers? Help me get the sights and sounds from yesterday out of my mind. Why couldn't you have saved him from the cross? Why did he have to suffer? What's going to happen to me now?*

We've all sat in crucifixion moments. Some of us try to escape others like Mary Magdalene face the pain and endure the agony and fear without self-medicating, blaming others, or running away. Pain is hard, and we want to flee from it. Watching your friend get killed isn't easy. Getting divorced isn't easy. Experiencing someone you love dying isn't easy. Losing your job isn't easy. Knowing your child is being bullied isn't easy. So much of life isn't easy. So much of life does not feel good. Life brings us crucifixion moment after crucifixion moment.

It's likely that Mary Magdalene probably didn't get what she wanted at that moment on the hill at Calvary. She probably hadn't gotten what she wanted in her life leading up to that moment either.

Scholars do not have enough solid evidence, biblical, archaeological, or otherwise, to have a full understanding of Mary Magdalene's life before she met Jesus, before she had encountered him crucified and risen. Like us, Mary Magdalene probably had moments of disappointment. Since her life did not follow the trajectory of a typical Jewish girl, she probably prayed desperately for more of a normal life. She likely felt pressured by society, her religion, and her family. Perhaps she prayerfully approached God, asking for what would have been typical of Jewish females at that time.

Those unanswered prayers of hers would become a gift. A gift to Jesus because her untraditional path permitted her to accompany him to his death and provide him with companionship at his darkest hour. To listen and witness his storytelling. Her unanswered prayers allowed her to be present at the tomb and be the first person to proclaim the resurrection of Jesus. By not being attached to a family, which would have been the expected path for a first century Jewish girl, she was allowed to support and be a close follower of Jesus. By not remaining in her hometown, marrying, and having children, she was there at the foot of the cross, a familiar face amidst the agony of Christ's crucifixion. She was able to be at the empty tomb, and from her lips, the resurrection of Jesus was proclaimed for the first time. Those full lips spread the joyful news of the resurrected Christ. That's likely a prayer not she (or anyone) would even consider asking of God. Yet, because of her untraditional life and trajectory, she changed the course of human history for millions of Christians.

She stands in contrast to the stories we hear about other followers of Jesus.

After Jesus' arrest, most of his followers went into hiding. Scripture tells us they even locked the doors! They were afraid. Their friend, their leader, Jesus, had just been killed; they didn't want to die, too! There was Peter who, for his own safety and self-interest, denied even knowing Jesus, let alone admitting to being one of his followers. Mary Magdalene does not lock herself away, but she was there physically and visibly committed to Jesus during his preaching, at the foot of the cross, and at his tomb. Perhaps she was scared, confused, and maybe even angry at or bewildered by those who had fled in Jesus' hour of need.

Despite being miscast for centuries, Mary Magdalene takes on a significant role in the story of Jesus and his resurrection. She is a saint in the Catholic Church, and the life she actually lived was likely far from the life she or her Jewish parents expected her to live. God had great and wonderful things in store for her. That is true for all of us. We limit ourselves. God doesn't limit us. God offers and extends opportunities, gifts, and moments for us to step into. We don't have to. The Bible gives us examples of people who chose both options.

We can be inspired by the example of Mary Magdalene remaining at the cross through a gruesome crucifixion and proclaiming the resurrected Christ during uncertain times. We can be reminded of how it's common for one's faith to waver by the stories of Peter. Peter denies knowing Jesus, let alone being one of his followers. Peter is rebuked by Jesus and called Satan because of Peter's limited understanding of Jesus' ways.

What we want or pray for is our own human longing and imagining. We may be striving for something holy, but our humanity limits us—our narrowness. God can call us beyond that. We are called into crucifixion moments as well as confusing but miraculous resurrection moments. Both are offered to us. Both are an invitation to learn and experience the ways of God rather than our own.

Getting an invitation is easy. Responding with a "yes" can sometimes be difficult. Sometimes like Mary Magdalene, we step into the opportunities offered to us, and in other moments we step back from or deny them like Peter.

We are likely not all "Peter" or "Mary Magdalene." Our faith, courage, and confidence may ebb and flow. Perhaps by being aware of the constant undercurrent of God's support and unending offering of the gift of unanswered prayers, we can confidently respond to God by saying, "This isn't what I expected, but I have faith in your guidance. With your help, I trust myself to step into and sit through crucifixion moments to get to the joyful resurrection."

Date: 04/13/2018 | Placement: Down the center of spine | Tattoo
Artist: Aura Dalian | Elements: Nepali script "Be grateful. Be kind.
Do the next right thing." Compass. Moon Phases. Planet Earth.

BE GRATEFUL. BE KIND.
DO THE NEXT RIGHT THING

Paul

As I look back at how this chapter of my life began, learning that my health was compromised and that my marriage was over, I can't help but marvel at how the conversations with my higher power evolved over time from, "Hey God, you've got to be freakin' kidding me..." to "Thank you, sweet baby, Jesus – once again – for prayers not answered."

As I reflect upon my journey, I marvel with gratitude at the incredible kindness, love, and support I received from so many and with disappointment and a twinge of regret at my contribution towards the devastation I both created and endured as a result of the desertion of others. I've learned a lot and am still learning. In my quest for healing and understanding, I learned degrees of acceptance, forgiveness, humility, and to not take myself so darned seriously.

I know I didn't have to travel all the way to Israel to reconnect with God, but I'm glad I did. My time in the Himalayas and the Amazon, San Francisco, and New York, and all points in-between, gifted me opportunities to interact with and be taught by so many people, places, and things.

Whether it was the Karmapa Lama or the beggar in Nepal, the Shaman or the environmental activist in Bolivia, the esteemed Doctor or the dominatrix in the United States – my family, friends, the friends of friends, and the many people I've never met who sent me kind wishes, love, healing energy, and included me in their thoughts and prayers...if you're reading this, thank you! In my quest for healing and understanding, you gifted me a prescription for health, a blueprint for abundant living.

I think what surprised me the most was that though my quest for a cure took me to the four corners of the globe to meet with as diverse a group of healers as I could possibly find, the counsel each gave me was, at its essence, exactly the same.

It's so elegantly simple, the application of which whilst not easy, promises incredible rewards. If adopted in the prescribed manner, it is potentially the greatest strategic enabler available to us all when it comes to reliably and recurrently produce tangible results in business and life. It is... "Be grateful. Be kind. Do the next right thing."

Likely by now, we're all familiar with the science that confirms beyond a shadow of a doubt that when we're grateful, we enter a state of psycho-physiological coherence. In other words, our psychological (mental and emotional) and physiological (bodily) processes get in sync, and we experience greater emotional stability, have increased mental clarity, and improve cognitive function. So when we're grateful, our body and brain work better, we feel better, we perform better, and we're healthier.

It was pretty easy to get into the habit of being grateful. All I had to do was slow down and take the time to acknowledge, focus on, and appreciate the experiences, people, places, relationships, and things for which I'm grateful. I discovered that it's impossible to be grateful and grumpy at the same time. Being grateful does wonders for my mood. People are more likely to want to play nicely with me, which profoundly impacts my immune system.

Being kind was a little more challenging than I'd initially expected, as there were two elements to this. Being kind to others was pretty easy. Being kind to myself consistently, especially when it meant only doing the things and being in the ways that would nurture and heal me, took some learning, getting used to, and practice. Choosing to eat healthily, exercise regularly, pray and meditate daily, get enough sleep, be responsible for my commitments and my mood, maintain healthy boundaries in personal and professional relationships isn't always easy but it seems to be easier and way more productive in the long run than not doing so is.

Just doing the next right thing was a little challenging too. It took me a while to get comfortable with the notion that I didn't always have to swing for the bleachers. More often than not, simple base hits will pretty reliably move me towards wherever it is I'm trying to go. I often chuckle when looking to do the next right thing. I realize that often the most powerful thing I can do, the most productive action I can take, is to pause and not do anything.

Doing the next right thing can be as simple and as easy as it sounds if we're willing and able to do what it takes to be and act in the ways that take care of who and what we truly care about. Before doing anything, I often benefit from asking myself, *Am I looking to be right, or am I looking to be happy?*

As we navigate the largely uncharted days of our lives that lay ahead of each and every one of us, we find a landscape loaded with risks and opportunities. Some we can see, most we can't. Inevitably for as long as we're still breathing, shit is going to happen. The good news is that more often than not if we're willing to, we're able to choose how we respond to it by whatever meaning we choose to place upon it — and how we choose to be and what we choose to do as a result of it all.

Whenever the proverbial shit hits the fan, we need to take a moment to breathe and find something about the situation at hand for which we can be grateful. Then, find someone in the situation (yourself or someone else) to be kind to. Then, finally, the next right thing to be and do will become apparent.

I'm not claiming that doing the next right thing will be easy. I am, however, offering that when we adopt: *Be grateful. Be kind. Do the next right thing,* as our default modus operandi; we'll have grasped a strategic and operational advantage in the face of whatever shows up in our lives. Having the willingness and the ability to be who we aspire to be whilst doing the next right thing on a consistent basis will keep us moving towards achieving what we're trying to achieve and taking care of who and what we care about as we go about living our lives in the ways that we want to live them.

When I look at my tattoo, the moon elements remind me of the cycle of life; we're born, we live, then we die. None of us get out of here alive. It represents to me the consistency and inevitability of change. New beginnings are always right around the corner. It also reminds me that indisputably unseen energy runs through us and connects us all. Just ask a teacher, an ER nurse, or a quantum physicist what happens during a full moon.

The planet Earth element of my tattoo reminds me that we are all interconnected on this great and beautiful orb. What each of us thinks and does or doesn't do affects every aspect of the entire planet and each and every one of her inhabitants. We are our neighbors' keepers.

The compass element in my tattoo reminds me there are tools that will help guide me, helping me to keep heading in the right direction. I don't have to try to navigate life blindly or alone. It reminds me that not all who wander are lost. At a more symbolic level. I chose a compass rose to represent spiritual direction, awakening, and discovery. It points to the infinite possibilities for interpretation of the past and choices in the present and the future.

The Nepali script down my spine is a reminder of my experiences and my declaration of how I am committed to living my life. "Be grateful. Be kind. Do the next right thing."

Rebecca

Wait! Pluto is no longer a planet? The model of the solar system I made in third grade is no longer valid? That planetary mnemonic phrase I used to memorize the order of the planets has to be edited? How can this be?

Things change.

No matter whether you are in outer space or your living room, things change!

Resistance to this fact can be problematic and painful. I know because this was a slow lesson for me to learn. I have come to learn that once you start to expect and even anticipate change, life becomes much more manageable.

The celestial tattoos of the Earth and the phases of the moon on Paul's back remind me that there's so much beyond what I see and encounter daily. Our planet, the universe, the moon, all of these things exist in the darkness of outer space. When I stop and think about that, it feels kind of scary. We are literally living our lives out on a rock that is slowly rotating around in our expansive solar system. Luckily, the words attached to these images on Paul's back, "Be grateful. Be kind. Do the next right thing," provide simple, easy-to-follow instructions for navigating life and, dare I say, the universe, no matter what changes come our way.

Beauty can be found in the thought that no matter what phase the moon is in, it is always there and orbiting the earth. Even in its small waning crescent phase, it continues to do its job and keep our planet in place. The moon holds us (the Earth) steady. The moon's gravity is responsible for keeping the Earth in its position in the universe. However, like us, the moon is not always the same. The phases of the moon indicate times of growth and decline. Similar to our lives, it's a continual, seemingly infinite cycle of waxing and waning, ebbing and flowing.

Just like the moon, there are phases to our lives. Different areas take focus depending on the year, the season, or even the decade in which we live.

Sometimes parts of my life seem like a different lifetime! Almost like they took place in a galaxy far, far away. What I didn't realize, or what took me some time to learn, is that things will inevitably change. For most of my life I've preferred to hang onto what is familiar in my life without much desire to change anything except my hair.

No matter what phase of life you are in it will change. Sometimes, God calls and beckons us to go places we don't want to go. Sometimes, God calls and beckons us to go places we don't want to go. A second divorce? You can keep that phase. For that matter, keep the first divorce too. Not being able to make ends meet, I don't want that phase either. There are moments when it can feel as though there is nothing in life to be grateful for. You get a large tax bill, a person you loved dearly has died, you've been living amidst a global pandemic for over a year, the person you love doesn't love you back, and you got fired. That really sucks and is not how you wanted things to go. Still, there is something to be grateful for in each of those heart-wrenching predicaments. God is bringing us out of one phase and into another.

The moon cycles through its phases without emitting any light. The "moonlight" that reaches us isn't coming directly from the moon itself. The moonlight we see at night is the sun's light reflecting off the moon's surface. Much like the light of God dwells in each of us and is reflected into the world and the lives of others through our own life, the moon provides a surface off which the sun is reflected. By being grateful, kind, and doing the next right thing, we are living a life in which God's love and grace are reflected off of us. This is an endless and continual event for both humanity and the moon. The NIV translation of Psalm 89:37 says, "Like the moon, it shall be established forever; it shall stand firm while the skies endure." God's light and moonlight will endure.

Doing the next right thing is like our own compass. The image of the compass amidst the phases of the moon tattooed on Paul's back prompts us to head in the right direction regardless of what phase we are in. Doing what is right is where we are continually prompted to dwell. It is our true north.

A compass works because the Earth is a gigantic magnet. At each end of the Earth, there are magnetic poles. A compass always points to the magnetic North Pole. The magnetic North Pole is not the same as the geographic North Pole. In fact, the magnetic North Pole can be found about 1,000 miles south of the geographic North Pole. When using a compass, you have to make adjustments to find the true north. Our true north is God. There are times when we forget to make adjustments to keep our lives and our decisions pointed towards God. We can get lazy or pressured by others to take a different route to lose our orientation towards God. The good news is that the new moon of our life can come at any time. We can adjust and reorient ourselves towards the love and grace of God at any moment. In each day and phase of your life, find moments to be grateful, be kind to others and yourself, and do the next right thing. This will ensure that you're pointed towards your true north.

Regardless of whether it is a full moon or a new moon, be grateful, be kind, and do the next right thing.

Regardless if you are in an urban metropolis or far off the beaten path, be grateful, be kind and do the next right thing.

If you're celebrating, be grateful, be kind, and do the next right thing.

If you are grieving, be grateful, be kind, and do the next right thing.

If you are hangry, be grateful, be kind, and do the next right thing. And go make yourself a sandwich!

Date: 01/11/2019 | Placement: Right chest. | Art: Gabriel Wolffe from Hebrew Tattoos | Artist: Aura Dalian | "Peace of God. Joy of Life." Elements: Hebrew script "Peace of God. Joy of Life." in the shape of a dove.

PEACE OF GOD. JOY OF LIFE

Paul

By the time I got to January 2019, I was confident that the worst was behind me and that my healing was well underway. I'd gotten by with a lot of help from my friends. In the last year or so, I'd been humbled, humiliated, and broken down. At my lowest point physically, I'd laid crumpled on the floor in the shower because I just couldn't stand up, in part because I couldn't figure out how to, in part because I just physically couldn't do it, and in part, because I really wasn't sure that I wanted to keep getting back up. Emotionally, I'd died a death each and every time I saw and felt the hurt and suffering that my poor health and impending divorce was having upon my children. Coupled with what was going on with my health, I was close to being done. There had been so many moments over the last year when I'd been so perplexed that, frankly, I didn't know if I was shot, shagged, or snake bit.

When I say, "I'd gotten by with a lot of help from my friends," I mean it. I would not be here today without the love and support of my friends.

There were my family and personal friends that stood by my side, supporting me in whatever ways they were able to.

There were my friends who I barely knew and some I didn't know, people from around the world who wished me well and sent love, prayers, kind thoughts, and positive juju my way.

There were my paid friends, the doctors, nurses, therapists, quantum physicists, folks specializing in applied neuroplasticity and epigenetics, and other healthcare providers who I felt had something to offer and could help me. And there was Toni at the HeartMath Institute, who helped me harness the power of my heart and the power of love. It turns out that there is indisputable scientific evidence that love is our superpower if we choose to harness it. You can measure it. Well, neurophysiologists, cardiologists, quantum physicists, and a bunch of other really smart people know how to measure and quantify it.

Last, but not least on my list of friends is a warm, close and very personal friend whom I call God. To me, He's not so much a Him as He is an energy. It's hard to explain, so I'm not even going to try. Let's just leave it at that.

My friend, God, was with me every step of the way. Sometimes we got on really well, and sometimes I was really pissed at Him. But, either way, He was always there. My relationship with God was the source of my strength, healing, and happiness.

I chose the imagery of a dove for this tattoo for a bunch of reasons. Quite simply, I like doves. I always have. I like what they represent. When I see or think about doves and what they symbolize, I like the feelings that arise. The biblical, cultural, and spiritual associations are devotion, faith, hope, gentleness, love, peace, and purity. Doves are a talisman to soothe and quiet our worried or troubled thoughts, enabling us to find renewal in the quiet of our mind, imparting an inner peace that helps us to go about our lives calmly and with purpose.

My primary reason for choosing a dove was because the dove represents peace of the deepest and most reliable kind. Regardless of whatever is going on, peace soothes and stills my turbulent, troubled, tortured mind. A peace that I can count on enables me to slow down the game of life and play it calmly and with purpose in ways that I'm able to take care of myself and who and what I care about.

Gabriel, the artist who designed my tattoo, created the beautiful image of the dove from the words (in Hebrew), "Peace of God. Joy of Life." I went with this design because, to me, the peace of God is that experience of inner calm and assurance that comes from knowing that God and I are on the same page. When we are, I believe that anything is possible, and a sense of serenity – and usually joy – settles within me, regardless of my circumstances or whatever might be going on in my life. So there's this very cool sense of well-being that *we got this*. So at these moments, it's an absolute no-brainer to me to do as Carrie Underwood sings and do what I need to do to let my faith win over my fear: let "Jesus take the wheel."

When I do this, first, there's a sense of profound gratitude as I'm clear that my peace is a gift from God. That said, I've come to realize that if I want it, I need to contribute to my experience of the peace of God. I can't be a jerk. I need to trust Him and be doing the next right thing in all my affairs.

I'm far from perfect. My cheat sheet for doing the next right thing in all my affairs is borrowed from my Buddhist friends. I find when I try to take the steps of the Noble Eightfold Path: right understanding, right thought, right speech, right action, right livelihood, right effort, right mindfulness, and right concentration, then peace and tranquility seemingly permeate not only my inner self but seem to be contagious, affecting others I interact with too. It turns out when we just keep on doing the next right thing, more often than not, we're psychophysiologically coherent (the scientific term for being at peace), and the energy we emit has the power to bring about similar changes in others.

The joy of life is a second-order effect of my relationship with and experience of the peace of God. As I've already mentioned, to me, the peace of God is that experience of inner calm and assurance that comes from knowing that God and I are on the same page. That, in turn, inspires joy and the inherent belief that anything's possible in any circumstances; even those that might at first blush look kinda crappy.

To me, joy is that feeling of confidence and happiness that bubbles up from within. It enables me to live my life the way I want to live it. When joyful, there are usually shades of gratitude, appreciation, wonder, and enthusiasm apparent and enable me to navigate and participate in life cheerfully. More often than not, authentic joy is visible, reflected, and apparent in our behavior. It is contagious verbally, visually, and with our energetic footprint spreading our joy out beyond us, affecting those who come in contact with us, usually in healthy and productive ways. Nowadays, before I step into the shower, I look at my tattoo, smile, and say, "Thanks God for your peace and the joy of life."

Rebecca

"How can you say peace be with you? There's no peace in this world!" exclaimed a middle-aged man dressed in a lightweight navy blue rain jacket. This loud disruption permeated the relatively quiet Sunday night church service. This man, who until now had blended into the congregation was apparently not experiencing the peace of God. On this drizzly Sunday evening, as we reached the part in the liturgy or church service when the presider says to the congregation, "Peace be with you," and those in the pews are encouraged to offer some sign of peace to others around them, this man couldn't keep his lack of peace quiet. He was apparently so peace-less that he couldn't help but yell out his disbelief at those gathered. It was almost as though he couldn't believe that we would have the audacity to say, "Peace be with you."

Until this point in my life, the sign of peace was just one of the parts of a church service. It was part of what we did, the rote ritual of worship. What came to mind for me in the man yelling about the lack of peace is that even though our lives may not be particularly peaceful, the peace of God can still be present. Our cities, country, families, jobs, and the news are not filled with peace regularly and consistently. The lack of peace probably permeates some of our days. Yet, each week at church services, we offer one another the sign of peace as Christians. Although I've been going to church for my entire life, the thought of the goodness that flows to me from God's peace didn't hit me until this man exclaimed during worship that there is no peace in this world.

The peace of God is beyond our comprehension. God is beyond our comprehension. There are things in our lives and in our world, communities, and families that we don't understand. They are 100% incomprehensible to us. I often wonder how people make it through their lives. How can they stand the stress and tragedy that confronts them? The overwhelming demands? How do they keep going with aging parents, schoolwork, school activities, a spouse's illness, getting fired, and more? Not to mention those things that continually go on at the global level. Poverty, immigration, hunger, dictatorships, it all seems too much for anyone to handle. Yet somehow, we do.

People have inhabited the Earth for generations. We, as humans, can clearly make it through hard situations. The more I read memoirs, listen to podcasts, and hear people's stories, I am astounded by humanity's resilience. We somehow make it through. We often have help, support, a person who listens and embraces us. I think that's where the peace of God is made visible. We are in a community with others. We get through life with the peace of God made present in our lives by the presence of others. Regardless of how bad it seems, God's presence is in our midst, dwelling in another.

Even though they are written in Hebrew (a language I don't know), I love the six words on Paul's chest, "Peace of God. Joy of Life." Despite being a person of faith, settling into the peace of God and joy of life is almost always a stretch for me. Some people can always have a relatively optimistic attitude, no matter what happens. They are able to be steady in situations and circumstances that would bring others (well, at least me) to their knees. However, I've discovered that there is such grace present in these six words. By embracing the peace of God and the joy of life, we realize that we are beloved children of God in a flawed, sinful world. By merely doing our part, living into who we are truly created to be, we can experience the peace of God and the joy of life.

The peace of God is present in the bad diagnosis, the divorce, the loss of a job, the death of a loved one. These horrible moments confront us, stun us, and often leave us not knowing what to do or how to proceed. It is the peace of God that permeates those horrible moments when nothing else comforts us.

These words scripted across Paul's chest amidst the image of a dove remind us that God finds ways to save us and gives us ways to save ourselves, bringing peace and joy. Think of the dove in the story of Noah's ark.

Whether this is an actual historical event is not important. What matters in the case of the dove and Noah is the truth that the story reveals to us. God is faithful to us. There are times in our life when it may feel like peace is far away. There are moments when we are being tossed about amidst floodwaters, but like Noah, we have to trust that God's peace is with us. God does not abandon us in these overwhelming flood water moments. Life begins again with the return of the dove with the olive branch. The peace of God is there and always was.

We read the story of Noah's ark in the book of Genesis. This story is God's attempt to save creation. Noah works diligently constructing an ark for his family and the animals of the earth. God clearly has a plan. God provides specific instructions for Noah on how to construct the ark. Noah gets to work and starts building. We don't know if he's ever built anything in his life, and now, he has been tasked with saving his family by building an enormous ark! No pressure, Noah. Once the flood comes, his family and floating zoo experience over 100 days living on his homemade ark amidst the abundance of water.

In Genesis chapter 8, Noah starts to wonder if the waters are receding. He sends out a raven and a dove to see if they can find land anywhere. In their initial flight, neither bird found land. Noah waited seven days. He sent the dove out again in hopes that the waters would have finally started to recede. This time the dove returned to the ark with an olive branch in its mouth. A sign that land must now be present somewhere and that the floodwaters were indeed receding!

I find it difficult to feel peaceful on a completely full three-hour long flight, so I cannot imagine the lack of joy and peace I would have felt on an ark with my family and a menagerie of animals. The peace of God came to the ark in the mouth of that dove. Upon seeing the olive branch, the joy of God must have been felt in the bodies of all of those on the ark. "Phew, land has been found. This is almost over. I was beginning to wonder if I would ever know what dryness feels like again." No doubt, like any good family road trip, there were moments of agony aboard the ark as well as some good old fashion bonding. But, amidst the chaos and floods of our life, the peace of God and joy of life is ripe and available for us to pluck and experience should we choose. Or we could focus on getting caught in the floodwaters of life and stuck in the middle seat.

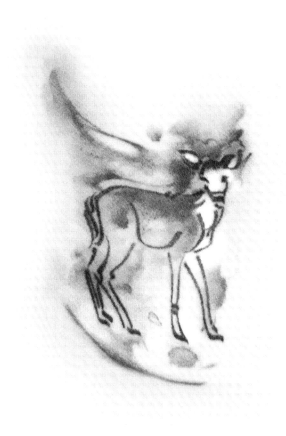

Date: 11/06/2020 | Placement: Right stomach | Art: Gabriel Wolffe from
Hebrew Tattoos | Artist: Aura Dalian | Elements: Hebrew script "Blessed
are the pure of heart, for they will see God." in the shape of a deer.

ERIN. BLESSED ARE THE PURE OF HEART, FOR THEY WILL SEE GOD *MATTHEW 5:8*

Paul

I am the proud father of three wonderful children. Jack and Kate are here with me in the flesh, and my daughter Erin is here with me in the eternal.

On June 27th, 2020, Erin had an absolutely fabulous day doing a handful of her favorite things. She went on a bike ride and a car ride with her mom and later that day went to the pool for a swim, where Kate and Jack joined them. That day she got to be with the people she loved and to do all the things she loved to do. That night, with her faithful dog Charlie at her side, she had a seizure and died. SUDEP, or Sudden Unexpected Death in Epilepsy, was the cause. She was closing in on her sixteenth birthday. I don't think I'll ever get over the loss. It's a cliché, but in a just world, parents really shouldn't get to bury their children.

There have been some days when I thought that her death was going to kill me. There are times that still sneak up on me when I think it still might. For the most part, though, I've done what everyone else I'd imagine does in similar situations. I suck it up, and, doing the best I'm able to, I move on.

Erin's life had been fraught with challenges from the time she was about three months old. She had intractable epilepsy and a gamut of other health and developmental concerns. That said, one of the many things that inspired the bejesus out of me was the way that she faced each day's challenges head-on without complaint and just got on with being who she was. She was smart, funny, intuitive, and extremely kind with a mischievous bent and an iron will which would sometimes show up as extreme stubbornness. She was also my daily reminder that adversity doesn't build character insomuch as it reveals it. Erin had a whole lot of character.

Three children in four years, Erin was the middle child. She had a great mom, brother, sister, and a dad who loved and adored her with all our hearts, and she loved us each back with all of hers. There was a lot of joy and laughter crammed into the years we were blessed to share with Erin in our lives.

There was a lot of stress and many tears too. Sometimes it was tough when Erin was alive. There were many and varied challenges and second and third-order consequences brought about by everything she had going on. Mostly though, it was what it was. It was our life.

When Erin died, and we were wondering what quote to use on the funeral program, Mathew 5:8, "Blessed are the pure in heart, for they shall see God," was unanimously agreed upon as it summed her up perfectly.

I've no doubt whatsoever that Erin saw God everywhere, in the places she visited and in the people she met. But, she didn't just see God; she showed Him to us too.

Though Erin was non-verbal, she was an incredible listener and observer. She could communicate volumes with her heart, eyes, and expression. I knew that if I could slow down long enough to truly connect with her energetically, to meet her where she was at, I'd be in for a real treat, and I just might get to meet myself as I truly was too.

Erin wasn't really interested in who people said they were or pretended to be. She had this uncanny ability to see through all of the insecurities and pretense that, to some degree, shroud all of us. She was able to see who we truly are and, from there, reflect back to us with pure unadulterated love who she saw. That was one of Erin's special talents and her priceless gifts.

Erin was also something of an animal whisperer. She and I covered a lot of miles together over the years with her lounging in her jogging stroller and me jabbering away in the background. My incessant chatter punctuated from time to time by her making the "Shut up, Dad." sound and pointing at an up 'till then unseen beautiful flower, bug, bird, bunny, squirrel, or deer. We'd stop, she'd go into her Erin zone, and then the magic would happen. I'd follow her cue and get really centered, present, and energetically coherent and watch the show unfold as the wildlife would inexplicably settle down too. It was as if they were drawn towards her in communion. On occasion, it'd be so beautiful that I'd have to wipe away my tears.

In the months after Erin died, I'd lay in my hammock in my backyard, having a wide range of conversations with God. It was like auditions for Noah's ark back there as wildlife from all over the neighborhood congregated to mourn and celebrate Erin's life with me.

When I told my longtime tattoo artist Gabriel about Erin's passing, he took her name, the photo of a doe who'd virtually taken up residence in my backyard, and Mathew 5:8, "Blessed are the pure in heart, for they shall see God," and created this tattoo for me.

Every time I look at it, it reminds me of her. It reminds me of who she was, and who she inspires me to be. She is one of the greatest gifts in my life, and for that, I'll be eternally grateful.

Rebecca

"I'm home! I saw a deer on County Y. When are we eating dinner?" This is how a lot of arrivals home were announced during my childhood. We'd walk through the door and announce the deer we'd seen, "I saw two fawns on the way home." Seeing a deer and being the first to share the news with another family member was like winning a prize. The first prize seemed reserved for those days when someone spotted a buck or fawns. This relaying of deer sightings remains so commonplace in my family that my nephew, Asher, had caught on as early as the age of six. He realized that he was part of a deer sighting family and would spontaneously announce to people how many deer he had seen on his car rides!

It would not be a stretch to say that I grew up in a family-focused on deer. Not only was my family focused on deer, but it seemed as though most of rural Wisconsin, where I lived, was also focused on deer. Deer were front and center. So much so that during the fall the small church we belonged to held a "Hunter's Mass" the opening weekend of deer hunting season. This Saturday evening, mass was held outdoors. The flux of attendees (out-of-town hunters who were showing up either to thank God for a successful opening day or to ask God for help in the woods Sunday morning) was so high that weekend that the number of people attending couldn't fit inside the small church building.

As younger kids, my parents (perhaps in an effort to get some quiet time) would load my brother and me into the truck for weekend dusk deer rides. They'd ride in the cab of the large pickup. My brother and I would be in the back. If we were daring, we'd edge our way to the tailgate and ride with legs dangling off of the truck. Our job was to look for deer. That was all. No radio, no screens, just the four of us scanning the rural Wisconsin landscape for deer. Our eyes and attention focused on the passing fields and forest, looking for one thing – deer. We had no agenda or motive in place other than to slowly ride around happily looking for deer.

The deer tattooed on Paul's torso, his latest (and last?) tattoo, contains Erin's name and a piece of scripture from the Beatitudes. Erin is the name of Paul's daughter, who passed away at the age of 15. I never had the opportunity to meet her in person, but I have heard stories of her from family and friends. Erin was unable to speak, yet it is clear to me that without saying a word, she touched many lives and is imprinted on the hearts of those who loved her.

The Beatitudes are found in the New Testament. Two different versions of the Beatitudes are presented in the Gospels of Luke and Matthew. The Beatitudes are spoken by Jesus in his Sermon on the Plain in Luke 6:20-23 and his Sermon on the Mount in Matthew 5:3-12. You may be familiar with them and might have heard people speak their formulaic phrases, "Blessed are the poor in spirit for they shall see God. Blessed are they who mourn, for they shall be comforted." These phrases make up the Beatitudes.

The Beatitudes offer us an inverted structure of the ordering of society. They encourage us to live differently than the world would have us live. There's a vulnerability that is expressed in the Beatitudes that I think would make Brené Brown proud. Counterintuitively, the order of things that Jesus presents during the Sermon on the Mount encourages us to be vulnerable. He tells us that those who mourn and struggle will ultimately be blessed. This, I think, is good news for all of us. Who has not been sad, has not encountered hardship, and has not felt as though they were lacking in something? The even better news contained within the Beatitudes is that something good, a blessing, will come from these moments of hardship. Paul's tattoo is one of the eight Beatitudes that Jesus spoke during his Sermon on the Mount in the Gospel of Matthew. The verse, "Blessed are the pure of heart, for they shall see God," is contained within the image of a deer inked on Paul's body.

The phrase found in Paul's tattoo and in Matthew 5:8, "Blessed are the pure of heart, for they shall see God," has numerous interpretations. The Greek word "katharos" is translated literally as "pure" or "clean." In this case, if we took this passage literally, we could understand it to mean that the heart has not been tainted, colored, or stained by anything.

When applied to one's heart, "katharos" can also be understood to mean "singularly focused." Just like my family can be solely focused on deer, one could center their heart and actions towards the single purposes of family, friends, or God. Focusing on God and striving to keep one's life free of hypocrisy, maliciousness, or selfishness seems like a worthy endeavor. Remaining centered and focused on God, maintaining transparency in our actions and speaking without malice or motive could be referred to as living with a pure or clean heart.

What it means to see God in this Beatitude is quite beautiful and achievable. We could understand "seeing God" here to mean that if one is pure of heart, they are likely to attract and live a life surrounded by people and circumstances that are blessings. Not to be confused with an easy life, but one filled with steadfast, caring, loving, committed people. It would be reasonable to assert that if one's heart were focused or oriented towards God, encountering God in others would likely come with relative ease. Seeing God, in this case, could become a part of our daily lives. In this sentence, Jesus may be trying to convey that with the right focus or "pure heart," we have the opportunity to see God in all whom we encounter.

As people, we strive to discover real blessings and joy, not merely temporal happiness. The prefix "hap" as in happiness or haphazard means chance, luck, and accident. We may think we are looking for happiness, but aren't we really looking for pure and true joy? The blessedness that is referred to in the Sermon on the Mount is not about money or good fortune, having a big house, or an Instagramable life. It is about the joy that comes from knowing one is a child of God. It's a comfort that comes from knowing you are infinitely and unconditionally loved and blessed.

"Blessed are the pure of heart, for they shall see God." From this one verse in Matthew's gospel, we can come to the understanding that by being centered and focused on God, we can have a joy that supersedes the haphazardness of happiness. This is the kind of joy that stays with us, just like God, regardless of the circumstances of our life. That's better than seeing a buck or a fawn!

EPILOGUE

Paul

I t's been more than two years now since Erin died. Whilst I was knocked off-kilter with her passing, the Earth kept rotating on its axis, and life went on for the billions of people with whom I'm privileged to share this planet.

Like everyone else, with everything that's happened, and is happening, in our world, I spend my days flipping between various states ranging from being angry, appalled, devastated, distraught, embarrassed, enraged, frustrated, heartbroken, sad, and scared. On the one hand, being accepting, ambitious, appreciative, filled with awe, confident, grateful, inspired, loving, resolute, and filled with wonder. So I've laughed and cried, lived, and loved, and muddled my way through each day as best I can.

All things considered, my children, the loves of my life, are doing well. I'm extremely fortunate on the work front insofar as I love what I do, and I get to do it with some exceptional people. My foundation is plugging along. I never cease to be amazed, humbled, and inspired by the incredible work that our teams do to enhance the lives of the developmentally disabled children and their families.

On the health front, I'm blessed and planning on staying that way. There are occasional bumps along the road, but for the most part, I'm extremely fortunate. My medical history will always be there lurking in the background that frankly worries my loved ones more than it does me. Sometimes I think it's an uphill battle for her, but Rebecca does her best to keep me on the paths that my doctors prescribe. It's sometimes quite a challenge for us all, as the marks of my past fuel me with an unquenchable appetite to live as much life as I can squeeze into and out of my body and to love, laugh, and do as much good as I can do with whatever time I have left.

As I navigate this adventure called life, I use my tattoos as a map to recalibrate against whenever I stray or get knocked off my intended path. I go to them for comfort, guidance, and inspiration. The ink and the scars, the memories and the experiences, the insights, and the lessons they each convey are an integral part of who I've been, who I am, and who I aspire to be. I've been marked for life. Thank God. Scars and tattoos are cool... they remind me that I've lived and inspire me to keep on living.

Rebecca

We cannot get through life unscathed. Life leaves a mark. Our hearts, our bodies, they take a beating. But, we also get marked by moments that nourish, strengthen, and enliven us. We have the opportunity to cultivate resilience, grit and become a gift of grace to ourselves and others as a result of the ways life marks us.

I once thought my second divorce was going to be the defining mark on my life. It seemed that it was going to be the end of me. I thought the circumstances that were my life and the obstacles that lay ahead of me were too much for me to get through. I believed that I couldn't have the life I wanted because he had left. Spoiler alert – turns out I can! With each circumstance (or mark) that life brings, we get the power of choice. We don't have to stay who we were in those moments.

I have the luxury of looking back over the past years, realizing how not succumbing to the victim role in my divorce or giving up on the life I wanted for myself has allowed me the opportunity to grow even more into the woman who I am created to be. If I had stayed who I was with my "no tattoo" dating policy, I never would have had the opportunity to meet, get to know, and cultivate the love that Paul and I share. The reminders of Mary Magdalene's faith or the daily transformation of the lotus flower that I get through Paul's tattoos would sadly be absent from my life.

Since writing this book, life has changed for all of us. The novel activities of the early days of COVID-19, baking bread, dining in igloos, and drive-by birthday parties, have waned. Instead, we are now adept at running Zoom meetings and wearing masks on flights.

It's fair to say that a global pandemic leaves a mark, but like the loss of relationships, jobs, and loved ones, we get to choose how we respond. God gives us the gift of choice. Sometimes the choices that face us are painful and difficult. Determining how to move on after a divorce or the loss of a child or job is likely going to be an arduous experience.

My faith tells me that God has created each of us for life. That is not to say life will always be easy or painless. It is to say that no matter the circumstance, we are cared for and loved by God. We are supported and sustained by God in ways that we cannot even imagine. We have been marked for life with the indelible imprint of God which gifts us grace and grit where we least expect it.

AFTERWORD

Paul

What if instead of being entrapped by focusing on what's happened to you, what is not working in your life, what you don't have, and what you see as missing or broken, you focus instead on what is working? Focus on what you do have and work towards enhancing it and being the person and doing the things that will move you towards living your life the way you want to live it, independent of your past and current circumstances.

I'm not sprouting some new age, pop-psychology BS. Rather, I'm inviting you to consider that, like Rebecca and me, you've had shit happen, and instead of letting it define you or hold you back, you let it crack open your mind and potentially propel you towards a future of your choosing.

I used to believe that my brain was hard-wired. That I was who I was... my words and actions declared to the world, "I am who I am, take it or leave it," whilst the small voice inside me, feeling like a fraud, implored, *please don't leave*. I was certain that life had molded me into being the person I was and that, for better or for worse, that was that. I lived out of a story that I was marked for life that my experiences, the consequences of my choices, and those made by others somehow defined me and my future.

I now believe that the marks, the visible scars, the tattoos, the invisible markings burned into my heart and soul don't define me. Whilst they tell my story, they don't necessarily predict my future. Who I am and how I am is not cast in stone? We now know with scientific certainty that our brains are malleable and that knowledge promises unconditional power. Change is possible. *You and your life can be the way you want it to be, independent of your past and your current circumstances.*

I invite you to accept that you are not entirely responsible for everything that brought you to this moment in time. But, right here and right now, as you read these words on this page, the good news is that you get to choose what happens next. Any combination of the study of applied neuroplasticity, our faith, basic common sense, and our own experiences inform us that desired change is possible. Regardless of what's happened in our lives or what's going on in them at the moment, we get to choose what happens next. If we want to and are willing to do the work, we get to live lives of peace and joy, marked by being grateful, kind, and doing the next right thing. The marks we've picked up through our lives are our reminders that transformation is our spiritual and evolutionary birthright, as is living our lives the way we want them to be, independent of our past and our current circumstances.

Last but not least, Rebecca and I wrote this book in part because it was cathartic for us, given everything we've lived through. We hope that by sharing our experiences and insights, you're able to relate to some of them and extrapolate something useful that helps you to get on with living your life the way you want to live it. Thank you so much for taking the time to join us reading this book. We wish you Godspeed.

REVIEWS

If you are looking for a better understanding of life, Paul Templer's and Rebecca Simons *Marked For Life* is a must-read. It is brutally honest. There is no sugar coating or bullshit to be found on these pages. It is in-depth, personal, sincere, and to the point. Glory, tragedy, happiness, sadness, success, failures, loss, and rebirth – survival. Survivors. Take the journey, buy the book, and continue on your path of self-discovery and self-improvement. One thing I can promise any reader is that you will no longer feel alone in the universe – this in itself is huge. Bravo, Paul & Rebecca. Thank you for sharing your lives.

Gary Guller | info@garyguller.com
Motivational Speaker. Athlete. Author.
Mt. Everest & Mt. Cho Oyu Summiter
The 25th Marathon des Sables (Sahara Desert Endurance Race)
Ironman 70.3 Hawaii
Founder: Make Others Greater (501c3)
www.GaryGuller.com

Disclosure. It would be fair to say that Paul is a great friend of mine. Also, I'm part of this book. You will find me in the chapter titled *Mary Magdalene*. When Paul sent me an early copy of this book to read, I didn't know what to expect. If anything, I was biased the other way. I didn't see it coming.

Warning: Beware, this book will get to your core and transform you. While touching on life's deepest issues, it is done with such a deadpan, unpretentious style that makes it irresistible. There's an entire page in one of the chapters where our protagonist is counting his many flaws, misconducts, and shortcomings; beware, for you will fall in love with him. Further warnings, this book will make you cry, it will make you laugh with joy, and no matter where you are, it will lift you up and give you hope. It is very likely that it will enlighten you.

After the disclosure and warning, here is my thoughts; this is a classic hero's journey rendered through 11 stations that mark a dying man for life. The hero is a pilgrim looking for salvation, so vulnerable he is he hides nothing from us, the readers. Raw and poetic, Paul's command of the language is masterful. Like Viktor Frankl's *Man's Search For Meaning, Marked For Life* is an instant classic. The co-author Rebecca adorns each chapter with words that are laced with grace. Her commentary is a relevant and necessary buffer between chapters.

Yossi Ghinsberg
Adventurer, Author, Entrepreneur, Humanitarian, Motivational Speaker
1981 Survivor of the Bolivian Amazon jungle (*JUNGLE* movie, 2017)

No matter how hard life bites, learn through Paul and Rebecca's experience that you truly do have the power to choose what happens next. Better than looking at yourself in the mirror, this book empowers you to look at yourself under a microscope… through the hearts, minds, and souls of two people who not only survived but also learned to thrive through some of life's most difficult moments. Paul and Rebecca, you are living proof that each of us truly does have the power to choose what happens next. Thank you from the bottom of my heart for sharing your journey so that others may also learn to choose and thrive.

David Folk
Co-Founder & CEO
NEXT Integrative Minds Life Sciences Ltd.

Paul Templer is, without a doubt, one of the most remarkable human beings I have ever met. It's hard to believe that a person who has endured so much hardship could be so positive and optimistic about humanity. His journey, both physically as well as spiritually, comes to life throughout the pages of *Marked For Life.* Paul is a natural storyteller. That is his gift. The way he weaves personal stories about adversity and overcoming obstacles into practical life lessons that we can all use to be better at relationships, business, and life — is simply extraordinary. Kudos, Paul, you are truly a rock star!

Ross Bernstein
Inspirational Business Speaker & Best-Selling Sports Author
www.rossbernstein.com